The Republic of Panama
IN WORLD AFFAIRS · 1903-1950

The Republic of Panama
IN WORLD AFFAIRS · 1903-1950

By Lawrence O. Ealy

GREENWOOD PRESS, PUBLISHERS
WESTPORT, CONNECTICUT

Copyright © 1951 by the University of Pennsylvania Press

Reprinted by permission
of the University of Pennsylvania Press

First Greenwood Reprinting 1970

SBN 8371-2806-4

PRINTED IN UNITED STATES OF AMERICA

DEDICATED TO THE MEMORY OF

LIEUTENANT GEORGE E. COOKMAN, USNR

LIEUTENANT (JG) FRANK FREELAND, USNR

ENSIGN JAMES KELLY, USNR

ENSIGN JOHN DUCKWORTH, USNR

ENSIGN WILLIAM B. J. CROTTY, SC, USNR

ENSIGN MARCY HARTMAN, SC, USNR

ENSIGN FRANCIS X. CLARKE, SC, USNR

* * *

Shipmates of the Second World War:

"They offered up their young lives in the noblest cause of all:—the preservation of the American freedom and cherished way of life."

Remarks made by the late General Alexander M. Patch, dedicating a Memorial flagpole at Calvertville, Florida Island, British Solomons, in May 1943, commemorating men lost by Motor Torpedo Boat Flotilla One, Battle of Guadalcanal and the Southern Solomons.

PREFACE

HUNDREDS of books and articles have been written about the Panama Canal and the Canal Zone, but very little has been published, especially in recent years, about the Republic of Panama. This dearth of literature dealing with the Isthmian nation exists not only in English language collections, but in the Spanish as well. Professor Dexter Perkins in his recent scholarly work, *The United States and the Caribbean,* notes that "Panama needs an analyst of the first order" (p. 239). This comment, from a very authoritative source, underlines the need. It is hoped that the following study, covering a limited area in the foreign relations of Panama, may contribute to filling some gaps in the historiography of this small, but strategically important, Latin American state.

Panama is one of the smallest of the American nations in area, and the smallest in population. Yet, because it is bisected by the great interoceanic canal and because it is located in the geographic heart of the Western Hemisphere, it is often regarded by military and naval experts as the keystone of the Inter-American System of security.

Although interest has usually centered upon the strategic military importance of Panama, there is ample reason for consideration of the Isthmian Republic in fields other than those of military concern. This work is primarily an attempt to trace Panama's role in the development of the spirit of international coöperation as a dynamic political force of the twentieth century. For the purposes of this study the concept of international coöperation has been defined in terms not only of regional developments, such as the Inter-American System, but in projects of general international collaboration such as the League of Nations. Furthermore, the record unfolded has sometimes even been a chapter in bilateral relations. Panama's part in World War I, for example, was not a case of action under Inter-American authority, or even of coöperation within the grand alliance against Germany. It was essentially an action undertaken in conjunction with the United States of America.

The record of Panama in international coöperation has, on the whole, been a favorable and heartening story. It constitutes a valuable case study of a Latin American state in the process of serving regional, as well as worldwide, projects of diplomatic, cultural, economic, scientific, and military collaboration for the common welfare of the human race. The devotion which has characterized Panama's long work in behalf of international amity, and the high caliber of the statesmen who have spoken for her in the councils of the Americas and of the world, have given the Republic attention, prestige, and recognition considerably out of proportion to her size and power.

In putting together the detailed information and drawing the conclusions which have gone into the making of this book, the author wishes to acknowledge the immeasurable benefits he received from the timely advice, constructive criticism, and encouraging guidance of Professor Arthur P. Whitaker of the University of Pennsylvania, his teacher and his friend. Many other friends and associates have given generously of their time and counsel. Mr. Edward Schuster of New York, author of distinguished works in the field of Latin American Law, although in ill health, gave his precious time and friendly interest to the writer and made available to him the resources of his splendid private library. Señor Carlos Berguido, Jr., Coördinator of Shipping for the Panamanian Embassy in Washington, and Consul General of Panama in Philadelphia, has also given greatly valued assistance and advice, and read and criticized the manuscript. Mr. Harley Notter, Special Advisor to the U. S. Assistant Secretary of State for United Nations Affairs, was also very helpful and made recommendations which proved fruitful in research. Also in the State Department, the author was given very great assistance by Mr. William Burton Sowash, of the Panamanian desk, Office of the Assistant Secretary for Inter-American Affairs, Middle American Affairs, Central America and Panama Division, and by Mr. Robert A. Thayer, of the Division of Civil Aviation.

Many thanks must also be given to Lieutenant Commander George A. Brackett, USN, to Lieutenant William Miller, USNR, and to Lieutenant George Busby, USNR, who used their own time and personal automobiles to take the author far and wide through Panama and the Canal Zone, and made it possible for him to study the country and mingle with all sorts and conditions of people. The writer is also indebted to a number of Panamanian friends who arranged introductions and interviews and extended the hospitality of their homes and clubs. Above all he will remember the friendly interest taken in his labors by his late Excellency, Don Domingo Díaz Arosemena, President of Panama and venerable statesman of the Republic. This friendship dated from the time of the author's service as a U. S. naval officer in World War II.

A word of appreciation goes to the attachés of the Archivo Nacional, in Panama City, where the distinguished scholar, Juan Antonio Susto, has helped to create an atmosphere favorable to historical research; to custodians of records at the 15th Naval District, Balboa,

Canal Zone; and at the Office of Naval Records and Library, Washington, D. C.

Officials of the Division of Historical Policy Research, State Department, Washington, D. C., furthered the author's work in many ways, and particular note is taken of kind courtesies shown by Dr. E. Taylor Parks, Historical Advisor of the Department, by Mr. Almon R. Wright, and by Miss Terrell and Mrs. Cross in Dr. Parks's office. The writer is also indebted to Dr. W. Neil Franklin, Mrs. J. B. Carroll of the Foreign Affairs Section, and Miss Kelley of the Central Search, all at the National Archives; and to Mr. Willard Webb, Stack and Reader Division, Library of Congress, Washington, D. C., for courteous assistance during long and fruitful periods of research in the rich collections under their charge.

There are many others who deserve acknowledgments, particularly various staff members at the Instituto Nacional, in Panama City, the Library of the Panama Canal at Balboa Heights, the Library of the City of New York, the Library of the Philadelphia Regional Inter-American Center, the Libraries of the University of Pennsylvania, and the Thomas D. Sullivan Memorial Library of Temple University. Finally, but by no means least, grateful note is taken of long hours spent in typing and arranging the manuscript by Mrs. Helen Thompson Ealy and Miss Geraldine B. Snyder.

LAWRENCE O. EALY

Philadelphia, Pa.
May 11, 1951

CONTENTS

Chapter		Page
ONE	Panama: The Crossroads of the World	1
TWO	A New Republic Enters the Family of Nations	14
THREE	Panama and the Inter-American System, 1903-1923	25
FOUR	In the First World War	39
FIVE	Membership in the League of Nations	53
SIX	The Inter-American System, 1923-1938	72
SEVEN	The Hemisphere Faces the Axis Threat	88
EIGHT	The Isthmian Republic in World War II	105
NINE	The Pan American Movement Since 1944	124
TEN	Panama and the United Nations	144
ELEVEN	Present Day Problems: Prospect	167
Bibliography		186
Index		203

CHAPTER ONE

Panama: The Crossroads of the World

THE REPUBLIC OF PANAMA is the youngest of the American family of sovereign states. It will celebrate its first fifty years of national independence in 1953. The great importance of this Central American nation to the hemisphere, and to the world, is evidenced by geography. In the twentieth century the Panama Canal underlines this fact, but the Isthmian region has always been a pathway for the white man's transit between the Atlantic and the Pacific, ever since Balboa crossed the country in 1513.

The romance and glamour of history are to be found in innumerable places in the jungles, mountains, and palm-fringed shores of Panama. Christopher Columbus, Balboa, Francis Drake, Pedro Arias de Avila, and Henry Morgan move through the pages of the colonial era, and the wealth of the stricken country of the Incas poured for years across the Isthmus over the Gold Road from Old Panama to Porto Bello on its way to Spain. In the mid-nineteenth century the California gold rush started a new stream of traffic across this narrow bridge between the oceans, and Aspinwall's railroad, the Western Hemisphere's first transcontinental line, was finished before the end of the year 1855. For a time after the North American Civil War, interest in Panama lagged, but the past half century and a quarter have seen this ancient land of Darien once more become one of the most vital spots of the earth because of the canal-building enterprises of this era.

During the struggle of Hispanic America for independence several battles were fought on Panamanian soil. In November 1821, a local junta declared the region independent of Spain and voted to join Gran Colombia, the nation of Simón Bolívar. During the next eighty-two years relations with the land of the Liberator were spasmodic. On several occasions the Isthmus declared its independence of Bogotá, and frequently the local administration was fully autonomous. Technically the union was maintained, however, for most of this period, even with the original state of Gran Colombia disintegrating. The Isthmus did not reach a permanent parting of the ways with Colombia until 1903, although it was a constant center of revolutionary activity.[1]

Long political affiliation with the land of the Liberator did not leave the traces one might logically expect. It is a significant commentary that Panama does not have a pronounced "Bolivarian" tradition. It is not a "Bolivarian" state in the sense that Colombia, Venezuela, Ecuador, Peru, and Bolivia have been classed to be by eminent authors. Of course Panamanian historians make much of their country's link with the career of the Liberator,[2] and the outspokenly patriotic citizenry of the Isthmian Republic are also understandably proud of it. In the summer of 1926 the Government of Panama called a Pan American Congress to commemorate the Congress of Panama of 1826, which was largely instigated by Bolívar.[3] At this 1926 meeting a huge statue of the Liberator was unveiled in Panama City which had been erected pursuant to a resolution passed in 1923 at the Inter-American Conference in Santiago to thus honor Bolívar and to "commemorate his prophetic vision in calling the Congress of 1826."[4] The resolution of the Santiago delegates had stretched a point in history somewhat, for Bolívar did not actually call the Congress, although he most certainly had much to do with inspiring it.

Despite such sentimental reflections and activities, however, it is obvious that Panama differs from the Bolivarian group of states in many important respects. Not only has the Isthmus always been geographically isolated from the southern continent by an impenetrable jungle, but its physiographic position between the Atlantic and the Pacific has brought literally the whole world to its door. This passing of human traffic over its soil resulted in lasting heterogeneous imprints upon Panama's population, so that today they are very different, ethnically, from the peoples of any of the other Bolivarian nations.

About 15 per cent of the so-called Panamanians of today are what could be classed as Caucasian; some 10 per cent are pure Negro; and the remaining 75 per cent are a mixture of various races, including about 1 per cent Orientals, mainly Hindus and Chinese.[5] Between 5 and 7 per cent are estimated to be of principally Indian stock,[6] but this figure is very conjectural. About three-fourths of the population of Panama City, and a high percentage of Colón, is composed of West Indian Negroes. In the haunts of these folk the Calypso-type music of Trinidad and Jamaica is predominantly heard,[7] and the spoken language is an amusing mixture of Cockney, African, and the Oxford Dictionary.

The urban centers of Panama City (100,000) and Colón (40,000) are characterized by every color and creed: Orientals, Slavs, Jews, Negroes, Greeks, Italians, Arabs, Germans, Danes, Dutch, French, English, Egyptians, Turks, Armenians, Syrians, North Americans, and, of course, Spanish-speaking Creoles and Indians and mixtures thereof.[8] The third city, David (10,000), in the far northwest corner of the country is more nearly homogeneous, of Indian-Mestizo nature, and nearly all Spanish speaking. David is an exception to the usual interior community of thatched huts, ill-kept streets, miserable shops and *cantinas,* and crumbling old churches.

In David one can see old Panama—Creole Panama. Here is celebrated the festival of *La Cumbia,* with its picturesque dances performed to the rhythm of pebble-filled gourds or *maracas.* The city has around it the prosperous agricultural and cattle-raising Chiriqui Province, of which it is the capital. David is far enough away from the Canal Zone for its people to have escaped the lure of working for the *Yanqui* dollar, which has caused so many to desert and neglect the rich farm lands in Colón, Cocle, and Panama provinces. Coffee, banana, hemp, and rubber plantations are also important enterprises in the Chiriqui coastal plain.

Before the white man came there was a large native population on the Isthmus which may have been as numerous as the 746,000 persons of all races who inhabit the country today. The Tule, or San Blas, tribe occupied and ruled the Atlantic side from about forty miles south of Colón to South America. The Pacific side, just above South America, was occupied by the Guayami, who are disclosed by a recent Smithsonian expedition to have possessed a remarkably advanced civilization.[9] All of these prided themselves upon keeping their race pure, and although today only a fraction of their former number they still forbid white settlement in their country. They despise the multi-race Panamanians who make up the bulk of the country's national population and have managed to keep their corners of the Isthmus as completely Indian as any part of the Americas is today.

The typical Panamanian, product of heterogeneous peoples, is of dark complexion and light frame, loves gambling, cock-and-bull fights, and immoral *exhibiciones*. But he is courteous, artistic, passionate, romantic, music-loving, poetic, and intensely patriotic. Although he drinks a great deal, he is seldom intoxicated. He has demonstrated little affinity for the bourgeois trades and has largely shunned agriculture in his trek to get on Uncle Sam's pay roll. Middle-class occupations and businesses are monopolized by persons not of Spanish or Indian blood, but especially by Hindus, North Americans, Germans, and Chinese. The white-collar Panamanian of Creole ancestry usually goes into law, medicine, dentistry, engineering, or politics. A surprising number of government officials have been doctors of medicine.

Aside from the cities of Panama and Colón at the terminals of the railroad and canal crossing the Isthmus, and the David area, most of the population of Panama is concentrated in the narrow, semi-arid coastal strip lying west of the Canal Zone—a region which is paradoxically called the "Interior." The people who live there eke out a miserable existence, for the most part, by farming and fishing.

Panama City and Colón are like another world from David, the San Blas country, or the Interior. The capital is a glamorous city of bars, shops, and cabarets. At night El Avenida Central, which runs crookedly through the city, is a glittering panorama of neon signs and lighted stores, while music and the sound of revelry come from the open *cantinas*, and a busy motor traffic of buses *(chivas)*, taxis, and private automobiles rolls along the thoroughfare. The number of motor cars is extraordinary for a Latin American city of Panama's size.[10]

The capital of the Republic is a city of many contrasts, from the dreadful slum quarter known as "Calidonia" (the heart of the West Indian Negro district) to the stately, palm-lined avenues of Bella Vista, where the homes of the Creole families and the embassies and legations of the foreign powers form one of the most attractive residential areas of Latin America. The public buildings, cathedral, churches, schools, hospitals, and theatres of the city are imposing, and the swank Union Club, overlooking the Bahía de Panamá, is the equal of Miami's finest. Traveling about the city in the inevitable *chiva,* one is impressed with the fact that the subjects which seem to predominate in the conversation of the typical working-class passenger are the national lottery, sex, and politics, in that order. The weekly Sunday morning drawing of the national lottery has become a near-sacred rite to Panamanians. Indeed, many North Americans have fought to beat the odds as well. One of them, an expatriated chorus girl down on her luck, is reputed to have hit the lottery years ago to the tune of $50,000—a sum she then judiciously invested in a night club along the Avenida Central, which became a favorite haunt of North American tourists and servicemen through the years and made its owner a millionaire.

Each year in the spring on Shrove Tuesday the people of Panama manifest the finest in their folklore and culture in the great Carnival Fiesta. Costume balls, float parades, "queens" of various realms for a day, dances, confetti, masquerades, decoration of buildings, and a complete suspension of business, add to the magic and glamour of this occasion, which is celebrated in every city, village, and hamlet. The national carnival song *"Mi Pollera,"* and the picturesque *pollera* costumes, reminiscent of Spanish colonial days, are never-to-be-forgotten sights of this gay season.

THE CROSSROADS OF THE WORLD 7

The Republic of Panama is a larger country than many realize, and has about the same area as the State of Maine. At the point of the Canal Zone the Isthmus is only about forty miles from sea to sea. The only break in the central range of mountains, the Cordilleras del Bando, occurs at this point, where the Culebra cut made the Canal feasible because the summit had lain only 290 feet above sea level. The climate is typical of equatorial lands, but nearly half a century of North American ingenuity, stemming out from activity within the Canal Zone, has made the entire country a fairly favorable place for Caucasian habitation.[11]

The natural basic industry of Panama is agriculture, but it has not even approached a desirable stage of development. The same is true for every manufacturing enterprise and extractive industry, despite the natural wealth of the country. The sad fact has always been that the lure of high wages to be had working for the "Gringos" in the Canal Zone renders it impossible to secure a sufficient labor pool to undertake any extensive development. Even when times are slack the workers will "sit it out" in their hovels in Calidonia, La Boca, or Colón, awaiting better employment conditions instead of striking out to attempt to earn a living from the land.

The recent years since World War II have been such a slack time. The typical crises growing out of unemployment have found no solution at the hands of successive Panamanian governments, and there have been many bitter expressions, among upper-class Panamanians and intellectuals, of the old view that Panama sold its birthright for a mess of pottage in granting the Canal Zone to the United States, and that the annual rental of $430,000 which the Republic obtains for the perpetual leasehold does not begin to compensate for the many problems which the existence of the Canal has deposited on Panama's doorstep.

One of Panama's greatest grievances, economically speaking, has been the resentment of her merchants over the existence of U.S. Government commissaries in the Canal Zone, which do an annual business of $30,000,000. The merchants quite naturally feel that most of this trade would come their way if the North American government would only close these establishments. Agitation toward this end has become one of the most complicating factors in the Republic's relations with the Washington government, and inasmuch as the United States clings to the belief that such commissaries are necessary to induce North Americans to spend their lives working for the Canal Department, no early solution of this problem seems possible.[12]

There is another side to this economic story. In peacetime thousands of tourists spend liberally in Panama City and Colón shops, theatres, restaurants, cantinas, hotels, night clubs, and commercial houses. Obviously most of them are brought to Panama because of the Canal. The United States Army, Navy, Air Force, and Civil Service workers and their families, when seeking a good time usually give the staid Canal Zone establishments a quick go-by to taste the "hot-spot" entertainment and recreation to be found in a thousand and one varieties in the gay cities of the Republic. The total of their expenditures by any reasonable estimate must run into millions of dollars each year.

The great tragedy of Panama's economy is that the Canal should have cast such a long shadow over it. The volcanic soil could be unusually productive for a tropical land. Where it has been attempted, the cultivation of maize, oranges, pineapples, bananas, coffee, coconuts, papaya, rice, cocoa, sugar cane, yams, tobacco, and mangoes has been quite successful. Yet the failure to provide foodstuffs in quantity has left Panama entirely dependent upon imports to feed the bulk of her population. During World War II, when German U-Boat successes threatened to get out of hand, for a time in 1942 there was a very serious tightening of the belt in the cities of Panama and Colón.[13]

The Isthmus possesses a great wealth of timber—cedar, mahogany, lignum, coco-bolo, and the soft wood ceiba—but most of the forests have never been exploited despite nearness to cheap water transportation. The difficulty again has been the utter lack of necessary labor.

The United Fruit Company and others have developed a small banana industry in Bocas del Toro and Chiriqui provinces. Some mining concessions, especially for gold, have been given to British interests. Aside from these the main enterprise unrelated to the Canal is fishing. The waters of the Golfo de Panamá are filled with seafood and are noted for big game fishing. Fish is the one foodstuff exported in some quantity, for the tuna fleet from the Pacific coast of the United States makes an annual visit to the Bahía de Panamá and takes away a very considerable catch. Very few Panamanians are employed in this operation, however, and the economic benefits are small.

Investments in Panama are lopsidedly North American. Aside from their mining operations, noted above, the British have also obtained some water-power, telephone, and telegraph concessions.[14] But figures on Panamanian trade disclose the one-sidedness of the *Yanqui* economic power upon the Isthmus. As has been noted, Panama is an importer of foodstuffs and of consumer goods. In both these categories the United States exercises a virtual monopoly of the Isthmian market. In 1947, out of a total of $75,704,205 worth of imports, $57,969,352 came from the United States,[15] and most of the balance was in foodstuffs from Argentina and other American nations.[16] Britain, a great producer of consumer goods, has never been able to break into this market. A British commercial agent in Panama City recently recited to this writer, between sighs, the utter futility of his efforts to organize some competition for North American consumer goods.

The Panamanian economy at this writing is precarious. The tourist trade has not as yet compensated for the loss of business sustained as a result of the demobilization of North American personnel brought to the Isthmus for wartime projects. A long-cherished dream for boosting tourist trade may be advanced if work is pushed on the Central American portion of the Pan American Highway. The section in Panama between David and the Costa Rican border is one of the most formidable gaps yet to be completed because of the jungle and mountainous terrain.[17] Almost all observers believe that an overland link to the United States would bring a tremendous increase in tourist traffic to the Isthmus.

The inflationary bugaboo of skyrocketing prices has hit Panama as it has Latin America generally within the past few years. Poor economic conditions are often dynamically expressed in political disaffection and governmental upheavals. Panama has experienced a great deal of both and, as will be brought out time and time again in the succeeding chapters of this work, the foreign relations of the Republic, and the measure of her participation in projects of international coöperation, have always been tempered by the exigencies of domestic Isthmian politics.

Footnotes

CHAPTER ONE

Panama: The Crossroads of the World

1. The story of the Isthmus of Panama prior to 1903 has been thoroughly explored in numerous works. In English the best in this writer's opinion are Gerstle Mack, *The Land Divided, A History of the Panama Canal and other Isthmian projects* (New York, 1944); Miles P. DuVal, *Cadiz to Cathay, the Story of the Long Struggle for a Waterway across the American Isthmus* (Palo Alto, 1940); Farnham Bishop, *Panama, Past and Present* (New York, 1916). In Spanish see C. Arrocha Graell, *Historia de la independencia de Panamá, sus antecedentes y sus causas 1821-1903* (Panamá, 1933); Felipe J. Escobar, *El legado de los proceres: ensayo historico-political sobre la nacionalidad Panameña,* (Panamá, 1930); and Ramón M. Valdés, *La independencia del Istmo de Panamá: sus antecedentes, sus causas, Y su justificación* (Panamá, 1903).

2. For example see an address by Ernesto J. Castillero Reyes, *Los Precursores Panameños de Bolívar,* reprinted in *Boletín de la Academia Panameña de la Historia,* Ano VI, Nos. 16 a 19, 1938 (Panamá, 1939). See also Octavio Méndez Pereira, Ernesto J. Castillero R., and Juan Antonio Susto, *Panamá en la Gran Colombia* (Panamá, 1939). This latter work is the report of the delegates from the Panamanian Academy of History to "al Congreso de Historia de las Naciones que formaron la Gran Colombia, reunido del 24, de Julio al 5 de Agosto de 1938, y a la Exposición del Libro, con motivo del IV Centenario de la Fundación de Bogotá."

3. George A. Finch, ed. *The International Conferences of American States: Supplement for 1933-1940* (New York, 1940), p. 384.

4. James B. Scott, ed. *The International Conferences of American States, 1889-1928* (New York, 1931), p. 272.

5. Guillermo Colunge, *The Panama Republic* (Seville, 1929), pp. 9-10.

6. Alexander O. Stanley, *A Geo-Economic Study of Latin America* (New York, 1945), p. 6.

7. Luis Marden, "Panama, Bridge of the World," *National Geographic Magazine,* November 1941, p. 592.

8. A. Hyatt Verrill, *Panama of Today* (New York, 1927), pp. 55-60.

9. Julian H. Steward, ed., *Handbook of the South American Indians* (Washington, 1948), Vol. 4, *The Circum-Caribbean Tribes,* pp. 44-46, 143-67. See also Matthew W. Stirling, "Exploring the Past in Panama," art. in *National Geographic Magazine,* March 1949, pp. 373-75; also Matthew W. Stirling and Richard H. Stewart, "Exploring Ancient Panama by Helicopter," *National Geographic,* February 1950, pp. 227-46.

10. According to A. O. Stanley, *supra cit.,* there is one motor vehicle in Panama for every 30 persons (p. 28). G. Colunge, *supra cit.,* who was writing in 1929, declared that there were at that time 4,000 cars in Panama City, or one for each 15 persons (p. 50).

11. A complete study of this subject is presented by A. Grenfell Price, "White Settlement in the Canal Zone," *The Geographical Review,* Vol. 25, 1935.

12. Clark H. Galloway, Latin Affairs Editor for the *United States News and World Report,* has an up-to-date and comprehensive discussion of this commissary problem, "Canal Zone Workers Like Their U.S. Shops," in December 3, 1948 issue of that magazine, p. 57. For a presentation of the Panamanian viewpoint see Scott Seegers, "The World's Best Business Set-Up," *The Inter-American Magazine,* August 1946, p. 12. See also Marshall E. Dimock, *Government Operated Enterprises in the Panama Canal Zone* (Chicago, 1934).

13. Edward Tomlinson, *The Other Americans* (New York, 1943), p. 144; also U.S. Navy Department, *Official Communiqués, No. 63* (March 26, 1942), *64* (March 27, 1942), *81* (May 26, 1942), *and 129* (November 13, 1942) (Washington, 1945), which convey the serious extent of German submarine operations in the Caribbean. See also Chapter Eight, pp. 116-17, below.

14. H. K. Norton, "Why Britishers in Panama?," *World's Work,* November 1930, pp. 29-32. *U.S. State Department, Numerical File 3626/1,* dispatch from Squiers, at Panama, to Root, January 4, 1907, reporting on failure of English railroad interests to get concessions on the Isthmus; *Decimal File 819.00/337,* dispatch from J. E. Johnson at Panama, to Lansing, August 8, 1918, reporting on dissatisfaction with U.S. commercial monopolies.

15. Thomas Skinner and Company, publ., *The Yearbook of the West Indies and Countries of the Caribbean, 1948-1949* (London, 1949), p. 646.

16. Howell Davies, ed., *The South American Handbook, 1946* (London, 1946), p. 623.

17. Carlos P. Anesi, *La Carretera Panaméricana, El Gran Premio*

de las Américas (Buenos Aires, 1938), pp. 115-20, 268-69. Also, Harry A. Franck, *The Pan American Highway from the Rio Grande to the Canal Zone* (New York, 1940); and U.S. State Department, *Treaties of the U.S., 1933-1945 (F. D. Roosevelt), Exec. Agreements Series No. 448, Trans-Isthmian Highway Agreement Between the U.S.A. and Panama* (Washington, 1945).

CHAPTER TWO

A New Republic Enters the Family of Nations

THE REVOLUTION which gave birth to the Republic of Panama in 1903 was born out of the vicissitudes preliminary to actual construction of a long-dreamed-of ship canal across the Isthmus. The idea of such a waterway had been recurrently considered since early colonial times. After the Wars of Independence the United States and Great Britain were vitally concerned and their interests often were in conflict in the Greater Gulf and Caribbean areas. The United States in 1846 signed the Bidlack-Mallorino Treaty with New Granada (as Colombia was then called) guaranteeing both the neutrality of the Isthmus and New Granada's control over it.[1] The Clayton-Bulwer Treaty of 1850, with Great Britain, was probably the most important negotiation of the first half of the nineteenth century concerning an Isthmian canal, and by its terms we agreed to share with the British in a sort of partnership any future project to build such a waterway.[2] The Hay-Pauncefote Treaty of 1901 marked the retirement of Britain from the entire field of a projected Isthmian canal (including not only the Panama, but the Nicaragua, and other possible routes of such a waterway), and left the United States free to undertake such a project as a unilateral action.³ This agreement may be regarded as part of the developing Parallel Policy under which the United States and Great Britain were to collaborate in so many of the critical areas of the war-torn world during the twentieth century.⁴

A French company, headed by Ferdinand de Lesseps, because of a combination of factors—malaria and yellow fever, unexpected costs in cutting through the continental divide, and failure to get additional funds—made a failure of canal-digging operations in Panama between 1878 and 1889. In 1903, after North American interests had purchased the French rights and installations, the United States negotiated the Hay-Herran Treaty giving Colombia $10,000,000 outright and $250,000 a year in exchange for a six-mile strip of land across the Isthmus. This treaty was rejected by the Colombian Congress because it felt generally that the United States was receiving far too much for too little.⁵

At this point the Panamanian business and political leaders, who feared that the United States might decide to build a canal via an alternate route through Nicaragua, staged a revolution against Colombia. These Isthmians were well conditioned in the art of revolution by the experience of a number of earlier uprisings. But this time they had the all-decisive support of the United States. Eminent writers have thoroughly covered this story of how the U.S. Navy and Marines prevented the landing of Colombian troops sent to quell the uprising, and how the United States recognized the independence of Panama three days after the Revolution.⁶ Professor Robert N. Burr sums it up very succinctly: "An outburst of regionalism in Panama, looked upon with favor by the United States, brought about the secession of Panama."⁷

The Hay-Bunau-Varilla Treaty of 1903⁸ between the

United States and Panama, whereby the North American republic received the Canal Zone, is also a general subject outside the scope of this work and already thoroughly explored by other writers. Reference to it here is necessary because its ramifications have had considerable relation to the role of the Republic of Panama in various projects of international coöperation within this hemisphere and the world.

The formal acceptance of the Republic of Panama into the international family of sovereign states was, like its abrupt independence, sponsored by the United States. The North American republic extended *de jure* recognition on November 13, 1903, when President Theodore Roosevelt received Philippe Bunau-Varilla as Panama's first Minister in Washington.[9] The next day the United States Department of State cabled as follows to all of its diplomatic representatives abroad:

The President yesterday fully recognized the Republic of Panama and formally received its Minister Plenipotentiary. You will promptly communicate this to the government to which you are accredited.[10]

This message started a succession of recognitions by foreign governments: France on November 16th, China the 26th, Austria-Hungary the 27th, Germany the 30th, Denmark on December 3rd, Russia the 6th, Sweden and Norway the 7th, Belgium the 9th, Nicaragua the 15th, Peru the 19th, Cuba the 23rd, Great Britain and Italy the 24th, and Japan, Costa Rica, and Switzerland the 28th.[11] Colombia was the principal holdout. Her indignation was unbounded, and not until 1924 did she formally recognize the independence of Panama and exchange diplomatic missions.[12] By the recognitions of the Great Powers, however, Panama had arrived, whether Colombia cared for the fact or not.

The circumstances of the Panamanian Revolution of 1903 created new anti-*Yanqui* resentments among many of the states of Latin America, but their sympathy for Colombia did not go so far as to impel diplomatic snubbing of the new Republic of Panama.[13] Every state of the hemisphere except Colombia had followed along in the parade of recognitions within a few months. Brazil established a full legation in 1907, and as early as 1909 she held out a special hand of friendship in the form of a bilateral Treaty of Arbitration with Panama.[14] Soon the Republic of Panama had widespread diplomatic and consular missions, reaching into every corner of the earth.[15] The vast merchant marine which the nation has acquired in recent times makes the consular service of Panama particularly important, and the Republic in 1949 had representatives performing such duties in faraway places like Shanghai, Port Said, Helsinki, Auckland, Hong Kong, Glasgow, Jerusalem, Oslo, Manila, and Capetown.[16]

On February 13, 1904, the constitution of the new state was promulgated, and the Provisional Government Junta, which had administered the Republic since the Revolution, abdicated. Article 147 of the Constitution, supplemented by Law 37 of May 4, 1904, provided that the Colombian laws which were in force in the extinguished Colombian Department of Panama on November 2, 1903, should continue in effect where not in conflict with decrees of the Junta, and with the New Constitution or the legislation of the Republic.[17] During the next forty years the National Assembly gradually eliminated Colombian law upon the Isthmus.

The new Panamanian Constitution differed from the classical North American model in that it provided no Vice-President, established a unicameral legislature, fixed the term of Supreme Court justices, and provided for the appointment of provincial governors (later amended to permit their choice by popular vote). The President was elected for a four-year term by direct popular suffrage. Provision was later made for a presidential succession by having several vice-presidents. The Assembly enjoyed biennial sessions and could be convoked in special session by the President. The Cabinet of five ministers served at the pleasure of the Chief Executive. He appointed the five-member Supreme Court of Justice for terms of ten years, but the justices could then seek reëlection by the public to an indefinite number of additional terms. Provincial governors originally appointed mayors of districts, and they in turn nominated magistrates.

The *Ministerio de Relaciones Exteriores*, a department of the government with which we are intimately concerned, was set up by Law 68 of June 7, 1904, which annexed it to the *Gobierno*. But by Law 29 of June 24, 1907 it was established as the *Secretaría de Relaciones Exteriores;* on October 1, 1936, its name was changed to *Secretaría de Relaciones Exteriores y Communicaciones*, and on January 2, 1941, it became a Ministry. The reorganization of the Cabinet by Legislative Decree No. 1 of June 15, 1945, again designated it as the *Ministerio de Relaciones Exteriores*.

On January 2, 1941, a new constitution became effective. This change in the basic law was inspired by President Arnulfo Arias. The structural features of the new constitution were generally like those of 1904, but a new provision which attracted widespread attention prohibited Panamanian citizenship in the future to certain categories of Negroes whose native language was not Spanish. There were two principal reasons for this clause—one cultural and one political. It reflected the views of the powerful cult of *Hispanidad*, which Arias represented, and which

Treaty of 1903, together with an unlimited right to take over any land or waters within the Republic which might be regarded as necessary to the security or maintenance of the Panama Canal.

These three concessions indisputably impaired the sovereignty of Panama, and to a degree were fiercely resented by the Republic's voluble nationalist elements. Yet I think it can be questioned whether they made of Panama any subservient lickspittle to Washington in the realm of international relations. There have been many times when the marshaling of states in favor of, or in opposition to, certain projects has been a matter of deep concern to the government of the United States. In this work I shall at appropriate points cite instances of Panamanian opposition to the United States, in the Inter-American System, in the United Nations, and elsewhere, which should establish definitely that Panama has been suffered to act as a free agent in conducting its foreign relations.

I use the expression "suffered to act as a free agent" because the fact is undeniable of course that the United States did have the power, and probably something of a right under the treaty concessions, to coerce the Republic of Panama at almost any time between 1903 and the coming of the Second World War. Prior to 1920 the United States did intervene four times in Panama's domestic affairs, but such interventions brought about no change in foreign policy, had to do with preserving internal peace, and in every case were at the formal request of the then Government of Panama. There were several occasions, too, when the United States obtained results by a mere threat of intervention. But these also involved purely domestic issues.[20] In the 1920's even this type of intervention faded gradually from North American methods. In the administration of President Hoover in 1931 the Washington government held aloof even when besought by various

Panamanian parties to intervene in order to guarantee a fair presidential election.[21] The slow drift of the United States toward acceptance of the Doctrine of Absolute Non-Intervention parallels its relations with Panama leading to the Hull-Alfaro Treaty of 1936.[22]

More often than not the Republic of Panama has found it to be in her own national best interest to support positions taken by the United States. This national best interest is a matter of economics. Because Panama is the "Bridge of the Universe" its inhabitants have given their major attention to living off the Canal and enterprises directly attributable to it, and are much too satisfied with this bonanza to bother about the very potential possibilities of their country's natural resources. They have made the Canal their lifeblood, and without it they would be reduced to a pitiful status economically. Consequently the Republic must coöperate with the Washington government in any measure clearly necessary to the security of the Canal. In the past the principal mistake of the United States has been in precipitately imposing its strategic conclusions upon Panama, rather than in allowing the Panamanians and their government to arrive independently at the inevitable decision that their own best national interest has required the Republic to support many policies pursued by the United States.

Footnotes

CHAPTER TWO

A New Republic Enters the Family of Nations

1. Mack, *The Land Divided, op. cit.*, pp. 133-34.
2. *Ibid.*, pp. 186-89.

A NEW REPUBLIC ENTERS THE FAMILY OF NATIONS 23

3. *Ibid.*, pp. 427-29, 552-55.

4. Mary W. Williams, *Anglo-American Isthmian Diplomacy, 1815-1915* (London, 1916), is a monograph presenting a detailed analysis of these developments.

5. DuVal, *Cadiz to Cathay, op. cit.*, pp. 170-254. The work by Dwight C. Miner, *The Fight for the Panama Route*, is noteworthy for its scholarly analysis of this background from the Colombian point of view.

6. Graell and Valdés, *op. cit.*, both present Panamanian views. Mack, DuVal, and Miner, *op. cit.*, contain comprehensive bibliographies, as does William D. McCain's, *The United States and the Republic of Panama* (Durham, North Carolina, 1937). Of great interest, but obviously to be read with caution, are Philippe Bunau-Varilla's own accounts of the Revolution and the events leading up to it: *Panama, the Creation, Destruction, and Resurrection*, (New York, 1914); *The Great Adventure of Panama* (New York, 1920); and *From Panama to Verdun* (Philadelphia, 1940).

7. Robert N. Burr, *Colombia and International Cooperation, 1920-1929* (Philadelphia: University of Pennsylvania microfilm, 1948), p. 8.

8. John Bassett Moore, *Digest of International Law as Embodied in Diplomatic Discussions, Treaties* (Washington, 1906), Vol. III, pp. 56-78.

9. For the President's attempt to justify what was denounced as "indecent haste," see Roosevelt papers, Library of Congress Manuscript Division, Washington, D. C. (Roosevelt to Moore, January 6, 1904).

10. U.S. Department of State, *Foreign Relations of the United States, 1903*, page 246 *et seq.*

11. *U.S. Congressional Record* (58th Congress, Second Session, 1903), Vol. 38, Part I, p. 471.

12. See below, Chapter Three, pp. 34-35.

13. República de Panamá, Archivo Nacional, Mensajes de Panamá en Washington, D. C., Hay-Bunau-Varilla, December 31, 1903.

14. República de Panamá, Asamblea Nacional, *Leyes de Panamá, 1914-1915* (Panamá, 1915), p. 127. U.S. State Department *Numerical File 6920/1*, Squiers to Root, May 27, 1907. Squiers said of this: ". . . her object in sending a Minister may be to observe the *North* American in *close* contact with the *Latin* American."

15. U.S. State Department *Numerical File 6920*, Squiers, at Panama, to Root, May 27, 1907, Disp. No. 107.

16. Carlos Berguido, Jr. and Jorge Fabrega P., *Manual for Mas-*

ters and Seamen on Ships under the Panamanian Flag (Philadelphia, 1949), p. 39 *et seq.*

17. Panama also ultimately recognized applicable Colombian treaties negotiated before 1903.—State Department *Numerical File 12980,* Squiers, at Panama, to Root, April 1, 1908.

18. An English translation of the 1946 Constitution appears in Russell H. Fitzgibbon, ed. *The Constitutions of the Americas* (Chicago, 1948), pp. 604-51.

19. Austin F. MacDonald, *Latin American Politics and Government* (New York, 1949), p. 618.

20. U.S. Department of State, *Foreign Relations of the United States, 1909,* p. 488; *Foreign Relations, 1912,* pp. 1139-40; *Foreign Relations, 1915,* p. 1210; and *Press Releases,* January 4, 1928 and July 27, 1928.

21. See below, Chapter Six, pp. 78-79. Also U.S. State Department Press Releases, January 3, 1931 and January 17, 1931.

22. See below, Chapter Six, pp. 80-81.

CHAPTER THREE

Panama and the Inter-American System, 1903-1923

THE VERY HEART of any study of international coöperation in the Western Hemisphere must be the Pan American movement, and the development of the Inter-American System. Examination of the foreign relations of most Latin American states demonstrates that this is so. Panama is a case study in point, and the story of her role within the Inter-American System makes something of a framework around which her diplomatic collaboration with others of the Earth's nations can be reconstructed for the purposes of this dissertation.

Panama, the Bridge of the Americas, has been closely linked by history and tradition to the Pan American movement. In 1826 the City of Panama was the site chosen for the Congress which was to a large extent summoned at the initiative of Simón Bolívar.[1] Then of course the Isthmus was an integral part of the Liberator's home state, Gran Colombia, and thus had no sovereign entity to participate *sui generis* in the historic deliberations that were conducted upon its soil.

The meeting in Washington in 1889 was the first genuine Pan American Conference, since there for the first time both Latin and Anglo-American states were in attendance.

At this Congress Panama was again represented only as a part of the Republic of Colombia. The same was true of the meeting held in Mexico City in 1902. The concept of an Inter-American Union of some sort was nevertheless watched and cherished by many intellectuals in Panama during these earlier years. One of the leading exponents of the idea, Dr. Justo Arosemena, whose works were widely read in Latin America during the later nineteenth century,[2] was in fact a member of a very prominent Isthmian family,[3] although his writings are generally listed in Colombian bibliographies.

Very soon after national independence was established an invitation was extended to Panama, through the United States, to become a member of the Bureau of American Republics.[4] On May 8, 1905, the formal acceptance of this invitation was conveyed to the U.S. Secretary of State, John Hay.[5] Earlier in the same year Panama had experienced its first taste of Pan American activity when the Inter-American Medical Congress had held its sessions upon the Isthmus in order to observe at first hand the sanitation and health program being carried on by General Goethals in the Canal Zone.[6]

At the Third International Conference of American States, convened at Rio de Janeiro in 1906, the Republic of Panama formally took its seat for the first time as a sovereign equal among its sister republics of the Hemisphere. José Domingo de Obaldía enjoyed the distinction of representing his country at this historic Inter-American Conference.[7] Señor Obaldía was a Panamanian of great distinction and was, in 1906, Minister of Panama in Washington. He was also Vice-President of the Republic at this time. He had been Governor of Panama under Colombian rule[8] and had joined the patriots in the Revolution of 1903. He was a native of the old creole province of Chiriqui, a Liberal in politics, and had always been immensely popular with the masses of the Panamanian people.[9] Within a very short time he was destined to become the second President of the Republic. No better choice could have been made for Panama's first representative at an international congress.

According to his official instructions Señor Obaldía was to work to have the arbitration of international disputes included in the Rio agenda.[10] He was also to favor codification of public and private international law, simplification and unification of consular laws, construction of a Pan American Railroad, and measures of public sanitation.[11]

As might have been expected, the representative of a small newcomer state did not play any conspicuous role in this third hemispheric conference. Panama's role, largely, was to go along with the general sentiment, and this included voting a resolution ratifying the principle of arbitration and recommending that all American states instruct their delegates to the forthcoming Second Peace Conference at The Hague to endeavor to secure a world-wide general arbitration agreement.[12] In fact, much of the excitement felt locally in Panama about this conference arose from the discovery of a plot to take advantage of the preoccupation of the government with the sessions and stage a revolution overthrowing President Amador, ousting Obaldía from the Vice-Presidency, as well as Arosemena, the second alternate, and installing the third Vice-President, Mendoza, as Chief Executive. This scheme was nipped in the bud.[13]

The famous Drago Doctrine was one of the dynamic issues before this Rio meeting. The United States was not pleased at the prospect of this conference furnishing a forum for a discussion of Imperialism, in view of its recent role in the Panama Revolution and also because of the doubtful reactions to the Roosevelt Corollary in Latin America.[14] From the standpoint of the United States, therefore, plans for the meeting had to be very carefully prepared. A close study of the proceedings leads to the conclusion that the North American republic successfully employed an old strategy familiar both to domestic and international politics: If it's not possible to beat down a movement carrying unfavorable portents, then by all means *join* it, obtain direction of it, and divert it as much as possible.

Luis Drago had originally intended his idea of the total inadmissibility of force in collection of international debts to be a rule of Western Hemisphere policy and not of the general Law of Nations.[15] He had refused to attend the Rio Conference because of the general movement spearheaded by his own Argentina to get the oncoming congress at The Hague to adopt it into International Law. The feeling of most of the Latin conferees at Rio was that the best protection for their states would lie in persuading the world body at The Hague to accept this principle of absolute nonintervention. As part of the Law of Nations it would be much more of a safeguard than a mere policy of the Inter-American System which might be dominated by the "Colossus of the North."

The United States followed a cautious policy during all of the sessions, with emphasis on the spirit of good will and coöperation.[16] Elihu Root, the first Secretary of State to visit South America, was present at the opening of the conference to deliver an address which praised the traditional concept of sovereign independence so dear to the Latin American heart, and took a tone of firm friendship toward all the participating republics. Perhaps the high point of his speech was an assertion that the Pan American movement should remain nonpolitical in fundamental character.[17] There can be no question but that Root made a very favorable impression which operated to soothe incipient anti-*Yanqui* friction. Since he left almost immediately for Buenos Aires to continue his tour of the southern continent he cannot be said to have worked at the conference in any real sense, but his address opened the way for the United States to assert its leadership and influence the definitive actions of the delegates. Although the United States certainly held no brief for Drago's Doctrine in its full implications, it went along on a proposal that the American states collectively recommend it to the consideration of the forthcoming conference at The Hague.[18]

At this point the writer feels impelled to digress momentarily from a consideration of purely Inter-American Conferences to follow the Drago Doctrine to The Hague in 1907. It seems most logical for the continuity of this work to treat next of that conference, in so far as it dealt with the Drago Doctrine as brought before it by the collective action of the Rio Conference of 1906.

Panama's attendance at The Hague had been doubtful. In October 1905, a preliminary invitation from Russia had had to be declined because of budgetary difficulties and the expense involved in sending a representative.[19] But in April 1907, this decision was reversed and Belisario Porras, a novice to diplomatic affairs, was appointed Panama's delegate to the World Congress.[20] His instructions were to ". . . declare that the Republic of Panama adheres to the principles of the First Hague Conference . . . uphold with all your power the principle of arbitrary arbitration . . ."[21]

The appointment of Porras was something of a surprise, but it appears that he was a power in domestic Panamanian politics at the time, a top leader of the Liberal Party, and demanded this opportunity to go into diplomatic service as the price of his support of the national Administration.²² This mission was, however, to be the initial service of Dr. Porras in a long and distinguished career in foreign affairs.

Developments at The Hague demonstrated why the United States had been willing, at Rio, to allow the question to go over to the world assembly. At Rio the United States would certainly have been outvoted in any effort to tone down the Drago principle. At The Hague the non-American powers joined the United States in modifying the Drago Doctrine by accepting the Porter Proposition, which greatly altered its effect by making a refusal of the debtor nation to submit to arbitration or to conform to an arbitral award a valid exception to the theory of absolute nonintervention. Dr. Drago, who was present at The Hague, made a long speech saying that Latin America would never recognize a right of intervention under any condition.

Although at Rio Señor Obaldía had indicated Panama's attachment to the general Latin American purpose of boosting the cherished ideals of the juridical equality of states, and had voted with the others to recommend the Drago Doctrine to the conference at The Hague,²³ the representative of Panama at the world congress, Belisario Porras, took a rather astonishing position and accepted the Porter modified Drago Doctrine without reservation.²⁴ Only Mexico, of all the other nineteen Latin American states, took this action. Samuel F. Bemis rationalizes this step by pointing out that Panama, after all, owed its very existence as a nation to the arbitrary intervention of the United States in Colombian affairs.²⁵ Nations, like individuals, are not likely to subscribe to clouds upon their own legitimacy. The action of Porras seems to have been foreshadowed by his instructions, which mentioned neither the Drago Doctrine or the Rio Conference of 1906.[26]

Following the congress at The Hague, Belisario Porras was sent to be Minister to Brazil and there initiated Panamanian participation in another very important Inter-American development, for he was also designated as the Republic's representative on the Rio Commission of Jurists.[27] The following year he was a delegate to the Pan American Sanitary Congress, at San José.[28] With all this experience he was a natural choice to represent Panama at the Fourth Pan American Conference at Buenos Aires in 1910. He was accompanied to that meeting by Manuel de Obaldía, son of President Obaldía.[29]

The Fourth International Conference of American states was marked by a lack of controversial issues. A proposal by Brazil to discuss the advisability of recognizing the Monroe Doctrine as a "permanent factor for peace in the Americas" was dropped because it most certainly would have thrown the conference into a turmoil of controversy in view of the current "Dollar Diplomacy" of the Taft Administration.[30] Most acts of the conference were routine. The International Bureau of American Republics was reorganized and renamed The Pan American Union, and resolutions were passed regarding customs, census, interchange of professors and students, sanitation, communications, etc. Of particular interest to Panama was a resolution directing the Governing Board of the Pan American Union to participate appropriately in the ceremonies attending the official opening of the Panama Canal, an event anticipated to occur before the next International Conference of American States.[31]

At Buenos Aires in 1910, as in 1906 at Rio, the small Isthmian Republic was not a conspicuous leader in conference affairs. Belisario Porras did, however, address the delegates on July 20, 1910, and made a well-received recital of the great strides in sanitation and control of disease which were then turning Panama from a pestilential hole to a tropical garden spot.[32]

In the normal course of events the Fifth Pan American Conference should have been held in 1915, but the outbreak of war in Europe and its increasing involvement of American interests led to postponement of this meeting, which was not convened in consequence until 1923 at Santiago, Chile.

This thirteen-year interval did not, however, cause the Pan American movement to become dormant. During the course of this time fifteen special Inter-American meetings were held, and Panama was represented at many of them. These included the attendance of J. A. Arango, Luis Alfaro, and Juan Navarro at the Second Pan American Financial Congress in 1919, and of Señora Ester N. de Calvo at the Pan American Conference of Women in April of 1922. Panama was also among the Latin American powers participating in the first International Labor Organization meeting, at Washington, in October 1919, and was there represented by José E. Lefevre.[33]

It seems essential at this point to consider a serious problem which affected Panama's role in the Inter-American System during all of the period embraced within this chapter: 1903 to 1923. This is the matter of the Isthmian Republic's relations with Colombia. No treatment of Panama's record in international coöperation could overlook this subject, for not only was the place of both nations within the hemispheric system affected by the bitterness of their bilateral antagonisms, but also the spirit with which they entered into any international project.

So long as Colombia failed to acknowledge the legality

of Panamanian independence the membership of these two neighbors in a system of hemispheric solidarity was an utter anomaly. Indeed the entire picture of international coöperation in the Western Hemisphere was affected by this circumstance, for as Robert N. Burr puts it:

Colombia's taste for the Pan American movement was soured by the Panama affair . . . [and] . . . From the time of the settlement of the question Colombia displayed a renewed interest in the Pan American System.[34]

As far back as 1906, rumors had swept Colombia that the United States was planning to split that republic further asunder by merging Panama, Antioquia, and Cauca into a new interoceanic state.[35] The Colombian sense of outrage over the *Yanqui* part in the Panama Revolution caused Bogotá to be suspicious of anything and everything connected with either Panama or the United States. As early as 1907 the government of Panama had sought to approach Colombia to work out a settlement of their common boundary.[36] In the detached atmosphere of Washington, Señors Arosemena and Cortes, Ministers of Panama and Colombia respectively in that Capital, did actually reach a rapprochement on January 9, 1909, signing a pact which would have submitted the boundary issues to an arbitration tribunal.[37] The treaty met with such a violent opposition in Bogotá that President Rafael Reyes was forced to resign in the ensuing uproar and the whole matter was simply pigeonholed.[38]

The settlement of affairs between Panama and Colombia depended fundamentally upon the success of negotiations between Colombia and the United States to settle the injury caused to the former by the *Yanqui* part in the Revolution of 1903 in Panama. Because of all this, Panama was a vitally interested spectator as the Thomson-Urrutia

Convention was filibustered for the better part of a decade in the U.S. Senate. The Thomson-Urrutia Treaty included the following statement:

The United States will take steps to get Panama to send an agent to conclude with Colombia a treaty of peace and friendship, to establish diplomatic relations and settle all pecuniary obligations between the two countries.[39]

As the Republican senators opposing this "Blackmail Treaty," as they called it, succeeded in prolonging ratification debates, Betancourt, Minister of Colombia in Washington in 1915, threatened Colombian withdrawal from the Pan American System unless the treaty were ratified.[40] He was assured that the Wilson Administration was doing everything it could to that end, but as the war went on the evident Colombian disaffection gave rise even to rumors that Bogotá was dealing with Germany. Colombia officially denied this, but some of her leaders continued to insist that only a withdrawal from the Pan American Union could preserve the national honor.[41] Colombia even joined the League of Nations with a reservation to the Covenant that her action should not be taken as amounting to recognition of Panama.[42]

After the Thomson-Urrutia Convention was finally ratified in 1922, Secretary of State Charles E. Hughes began a protracted negotiation in accordance with the above-quoted clause of the treaty to bring Panama and Colombia together.[43] On May 8, 1924, Hughes, Enrique Olaya Herrera, Minister of Colombia, and Ricardo J. Alfaro, Minister of Panama, agreed in Washington that the two Latin American republics would initiate diplomatic relations on May 15, 1924. At Bogotá on August 20, 1924, Jorge Velez, the Colombian Foreign Minister, and Nicholas Victoria J., the newly arrived Minister of Panama, signed a treaty which definitely and permanently settled the boundary issues, and was promptly ratified.[44] The two governments have since enjoyed most amicable relations. In 1935, 1936, and 1937, a joint demarcation commission worked in complete harmony in the frontier region. In 1927 the two nations made an aerial photographic study of the river systems of La Miel for the purpose of navigational aids. Today Panama is represented at Bogotá by a full embassy, and the tendency in Panama City is to regard Colombian relations as second to none—not even those of the United States.

The settlement of this bitter controversy removed one of the clouds which had long hovered over schemes for Pan American solidarity. It was an immense relief not only to the two nations most directly concerned, and to the United States, but to all advocates of hemispheric coöperation. Furthermore, it came at a most opportune time—on the eve of the first post-war congress, the oncoming Fifth International Conference of American States at Santiago. That meeting would be plagued with many other obstacles to peace and harmony within the Americas, and it must have been some source of encouragement to know that even one acrimonious intra-hemispheric dispute had been settled at long last.

Footnotes

CHAPTER THREE

The Inter-American System, 1903-1923

1. See Chapter One, pp. 2-3 *supra*.
2. Justo Arosemena, *Estudio sobre la idea de una liga américana* (Lima, 1864); *Proyecto de tratado para formar una liga sur-améri-*

cana (Lima, 1865); *Estudios constitucionales sobre los gobiernos de la América latina* (Paris, 1878–2 vol.).

3. The best biography of this distinguished Panamanian scholar and statesman is Octavio Méndez Pereira, *Justo Arosemena, 1817-1896* (Panamá, 1919).

4. U.S. State Department, Dispatches from Panama, 1903-1906, Joseph W. Slee, to Hay, November 6, 1904.

5. *Ibid.*, John Barrett to Hay, May 8, 1905.

6. *Ibid.*, Barrett to Hay, January 12, 1905. This dispatch is a report on the sessions of the Pan American Medical Congress.

7. República de Panamá, Secretaría de Gobierno y Relaciones Exteriores, *Memoria 1906* (Panamá, 1907), p. LII.

8. U.S. State Department, *Foreign Relations 1903*, p. 190.

9. U.S. State Department, *Numerical File 847/35*, Squiers, at Panama, to Root, December 9, 1907.—An Appraisal of Obaldía.

10. U.S. State Department, Dispatches from Panama, 1903-1906, William F. Sands to Root, March 31, 1906.

11. República de Panamá, Secretaría de Gobierno y Relaciones Exteriores, *Memoria 1906, supra cit.*, p. LII.

12. Gordon Ireland, *Boundaries, Possessions, and Conflicts in Central and North America and the Caribbean* (Cambridge, Mass., 1941), p. 394.

13. U.S. State Department, Dispatches from Panama, 1903-1906, Magoon to Root, August 11, 1906.

14. John P. Humphrey, *The Inter-American System, A Canadian View* (Toronto, 1942), pp. 57-60.

15. John Bassett Moore, *Digest of International Law, op. cit.*, Vol. VI, pp. 586-93.

16. Victor Andres Belaunde, *Latin America and the United States* (in Quincy Wright, ed., *Interpretations of American Foreign Policy*) (Chicago, 1930), p. 138.

17. U.S. State Department, *Report of the Delegates of the United States to the Third International Conference of American States* (Washington, 1907), p. 63.

18. E. S. Zeballos, *Conferencias Internacionales Américanas, 1797-1910* (Valencia, 1914), pp. 15-16.

19. República de Panamá, Archivo Nacional, Mensajes del Ministro en Washington, No. 12, April 14, 1907, Obaldía-Root.

20. U.S. State Department, *Numerical File 40/199*, Squiers, at Panama, to Root, April 17, 1907, No. 85.

21. *Ibid., Numerical File 40/241-242*, Squiers, at Panama, to Root, May 2, 1907, No. 93.

22. República de Panamá, Mensajes del Ministro en Washington, No. 13, April 17, 1907, Obaldía-Root.

23. James B. Scott, ed., *The International Conferences of American States, 1889-1928* (New York, 1931), pp. 123 and 136.
24. James B. Scott, *The Hague Peace Conferences of 1899 and 1907* (Baltimore, 1909), p. 435; and Scott, ed., *The International Conferences, etc., supra,* p. 135n.
25. Samuel F. Bemis, *The Latin American Policy of the United States* (New York, 1943), p. 229.
26. Squiers to Root, Note 21, *supra.*
27. U.S. State Department, *Numerical File 12631,* Squiers, at Panama, to Root, March 7, 1908.
28. U.S. State Department, *Numerical File 20272/15,* Weitzel, at Panama, to Knox, September 18, 1909, No. 561.
29. República de Panamá, Ministerio de Relaciones Exteriores, *Memoria 1910* (Panamá, 1911), p. XV.
30. Alejandro Alvarez, "The Monroe Doctrine at the Fourth Pan American Conference," *Annals of the American Academy of Political and Social Science,* May 1911 issue, p. 24 *et seq.*
31. James B. Scott, ed., *The International Conferences, etc., supra. cit.,* p. 170.
32. E. S. Zeballos, *Conferencias Internacionales Américanas, 1797-1910, supra,* pp. 223-28.
33. U.S. State Department, Dispatches from Panama, 1910-1929, tel. Price to Lansing, rec'd. 5 p.m., December 9, 1919; South to Hughes, No. 25 of March 7, 1922; Price to Lansing, No. 10 of September 6, 1919.
34. Robert N. Burr, *Colombia and International Cooperation, op. cit.,* pp. 141-42.
35. E. Taylor Parks, *Colombia and the United States* (Durham, N. C., 1935), p. 432. U.S. State Department, *Numerical File 4485/8,* from Squiers, at Panama, to Root, February 12, 1907, No. 55; *Numerical File 9271/10,* Squiers, to Root, November 22, 1907, No. 148; *Numerical File 5025/89a,* Squiers, to Root, May 4, 1909.
36. U.S. State Department, *Numerical Files,* all Squiers to Root, *4176*—January 25, 1907; *4176/1*—January 25, 1907; *4176/2-3*—January 31, 1907.
37. U.S. State Department, *Foreign Relations 1909, op. cit.,* pp. 229-33.
38. Leandro Medina, *Límité Oriental de Panamá* (Bogotá, 1913). See also U.S. State Department, Dispatches from Panama, 1903-6, William F. Sands to Root, March 7, 1906; *Numerical File 4176,* Squiers to Root, January 25, 1907.
39. U.S. State Department, *Foreign Relations 1914, op. cit.,* p. 163.

40. U.S. *Senate Document No. 64* (68th Congress, First Session 1923), p. 17.

41. Antonio Llano, "A Colombian View of the Treaty," *New York Times,* March 13, 1917. See also *New York Times* for March 17, 1917.

42. Burr, *Colombia and International Cooperation, supra,* p. 186.

43. República de Panamá, Asamblea Nacional, *Leyes 1924-1925,* (Panamá, 1925), p. 103. Also U.S. State Department, *Decimal File 701.1921/2,* from John G. South, at Panamá, to Hughes, May 31, 1922.

44. República de Panamá, Secretaría de Relaciones Exteriores, *Memoria 1923-1924* (Panamá, 1926), pp. 139-54.

CHAPTER FOUR

In the First World War

THE LAST full-dress parade of a world whose conscience still prodded it to outlaw the horror of war in the twentieth century was the second Peace Conference at the Hague. Here the Republic of Panama for the first time took part in a world-wide congress of sovereign states. With six other Central American and Caribbean nations the Isthmian republic on October 18, 1907, signed The Hague Convention "for the pacific settlement of international disputes," and for the creation of the Permanent Court of Arbitration. Panama deposited its ratification of these Hague conventions on September 11, 1911.[1]

War in Europe in 1914 might have been of little immediate concern to a small Hispanic American state in the ordinary scheme of things, but the year 1914 was the very year that brought the flags and nationals of faraway countries to the shores of Panama to a degree never known before. The Panama Canal was opened to traffic in that year, and the Isthmus became the crossroads of a world now involved in the smoke and flame of the most dreadful conflict ever known. It would not be possible for the Republic of Panama to be long isolated from the ramifications of such a struggle, and she was involved almost at once in problems that related entirely to the war swiftly enveloping the seven seas.

Any consideration of Panama's role in the First World War can be very logically divided into two phases. But both will be conditioned by the status of the United States, for the first is the Period of Declared Neutrality and the second is the Period of Actual Belligerency which followed the North American declaration of war in 1917.

The United States construed Articles II and III of the Hay-Bunau-Varilla Treaty granting it "jurisdiction" over the Canal Zone as meaning that ports and waters of the Zone would be subject to the same neutrality rules as the ports and waters of the continental United States. Consequently President Wilson's proclamations of neutrality in 1914, 1915, and 1916 were applied to the Canal Zone.[2] Yet in view of Panama's continued title to the land over which the United States held a perpetual leasehold, some doubt was raised concerning the question of the Zone's status in neutrality. In order to set aside every doubt an additional Wilson proclamation covering the Canal Zone specifically was issued on November 13, 1914.[3]

These actions on the part of the United States created some embarrassment inasmuch as the Republic of Panama made no proclamation of neutrality,[4] and in fact had no public statutes regarding the rights and duties of neutrals in time of war or of the treatment of citizens, property, and vessels of belligerents within its boundaries and territorial waters.[5] The difficulty for the United States in enforcing its regulations in the Zone was aggravated by the anomaly of the Panamanian position. The Washington government sought some arrangement which would make "one neutral jurisdiction" of the Republic and the Canal Zone.[6] An agreement, the Lansing-Morales Protocol, was signed at Washington on October 10, 1914, providing that hospitality once extended in the waters of Panama to a belligerent vessel should serve to deprive such vessel of like hospitality in the Canal Zone for a period of three months, and vice versa.[7] This naturally fell far short of the "one neutral jurisdiction" idea.

Incidents and test cases of these principles were few. In January of 1915 warships of Japan and Great Britain put military personnel ashore in Puerto Piñas while engine repairs were made aboard one of the vessels. The Panamanian government notified the two powers that it regarded extension of hospitality in the case to be justified on the ground that an emergency existed and that there was consequently no breach of the Republic's neutrality.[8] The records of the Panama Canal disclose that no German, Austrian, or Turkish ship actually transited the Canal after the outbreak of the war. However, six German ships did take advantage of United States neutrality to lay up in Balboa and Cristobal harbors.[9] Being merchantmen they could stay indefinitely and thus avoid the almost certain capture at the hands of British warships which would have followed their putting to sea. They were thus caught in the Zone by the North American declaration of war in April, 1917. By executive order of June 30, 1917, these vessels were boarded and seized.

It was urged by some that this action constituted a violation of the Convention of 1903 with the Republic of Panama, which stated that the Canal and its entrances were to be "neutral in perpetuity." However, this would raise the question whether a third power (viz., Germany) could claim the benefit of the solemn commitment made to Panama, especially when, as was certainly the case here, that Republic made no objection to the action complained about. A much more valid conclusion to be drawn from this episode is that the perpetual "neutrality" of the Zone will operate to protect only the vessels of friendly states when the United States happens to be at war.

Many Allied vessels entered Panamanian waters and transited the Canal during the war, but there were only two instances of disciplinary action—both against British merchantmen. One involved a breaking of radio silence and the other a violation of pratique regulations. Neither was a serious infraction, and the British government acknowledged the justice of the disciplinary measures enforced.[10]

The tone and conduct of both Panamanian and Canal Zone officials grew ever more favorable to the Allies as the war progressed. In the case of the Republic this was in the face of a respectably sized element of the population of Teutonic origins,[11] particularly in business circles in Panama City and Colón, and in the provinces of Cocle, where German immigrants settled in the mid-nineteenth century and have never been entirely assimilated, Chiriqui, and Bocas del Toro.[12] Panama shared with Ibero-America generally a sympathy for kindred Latin nations, France and Italy. Panama is an excellent example of the French-inspired Pan Latinist movement noted by J. F. Normano,[13] and traces of French literature, art, and way of life have lingered since the eighteenth century and were greatly strengthened during the period when the French New Canal Company undertook the first monumental effort to dig an Isthmian canal. In Panama City there is de Lesseps Park as a constant reminder of this, and one of the works of art most prized by the people of Panama is a gigantic statue of Christopher Columbus in the city of Colón which was given by the Empress Eugénie of France, a cousin of de Lesseps. Reports of German "frightfulness" in Belgium and occupied France heightened pro-Allied feeling in a country which still recalled the German bombardment of nearby Venezuelan ports only a few years before, and had sentimentally adopted Bastille Day as one of its own legal holidays.[14]

As the actual entry of the United States into the war loomed as a virtual certainty, the Republic of Panama allowed U.S. Secret Service agents free access to all sections of the country to note the movements of suspicious persons and to forestall any possible sabotage of the Canal or of other public works. In 1912 Panama had granted permission for the armed forces of the United States to "reconnoiter" in Panamanian territory, and in February 1917 the Ministry of Foreign Affairs advised that Panama would coöperate in every way to allow North American troops to operate over its soil in defense of the Canal and the Isthmus.[15]

The Wilson Administration was naturally anxious to have the isthmian government join its break with the Central Powers. In March 1917 John Foster Dulles was sent to Panama by Secretary Lansing to do all in his power to facilitate this.[16] He wrote: "It was not necessary to bring any particular coercion. Panama seemed to realize . . . that it would be impracticable . . . to maintain a neutrality."[17] Dulles further indicated that Panama's economic dependence upon the United States was the compelling factor in the Panamanian attitude, and disclosed that he had authority to promise the Isthmian Republic exemptions of all income earned in Panama from U. S. Federal taxes in return for coöperation in the war.

When the United States formally declared war upon Germany, President Valdez, on April 7, 1917, issued a "Proclamation of Coöperation with the United States in War against Germany."[18] The United States found this an ambiguous action and requested Panama to clarify its meaning. The Valdez government replied that it "considered the proclamation a declaration of war in its legal effect."[19] Panama had ended all diplomatic ties with Germany several days before.[20]

The Republic was now directly involved in the most gigantic enterprise the world had ever known—the Allied combination to crush the Central Powers. The whole subject of the maze of entangling alliances in Europe now touched this small Central American nation. Panama had proclaimed its participation in the war an act of "coöperation with the United States." It had thus hitched itself to North American purposes in the conflict. Since the United States had in turn publicly proclaimed that its status in the struggle was that of an "associated power" in the combination opposing Germany, and that it was not technically one of the "Allies," it naturally followed that Panama had placed herself in the same category by the statement of alignment with the United States. Perhaps it was a realization of this position of following along in the wake of the *Yanqui* colossus which prompted the Panamanian government to be unequivocal in its declaration of war against the second Teutonic power, Austria-Hungary, on December 10, 1917.[21]

During the course of the First World War there was some sympathy for Germany in Latin American nations which held traditional antagonisms toward the United States.[22] In the spring of 1917 Argentina, in collusion probably with Mexico, proposed a conference of American "neutrals" which seemed rather obviously calculated to embarrass the United States. Panama was invited to participate in this movement, but snubbed the proposal and made clear her solidarity with the United States.[23] Similar reactions from most of the nations of the hemisphere caused the project to be stillborn.[24]

Aside from giving the United States carte blanche to undertake any necessary military operations within Panamanian jurisdiction, the principal role played by the Republic in the coöperative enterprise of reducing the Central Powers was to crack down on possible saboteurs and enemy agents, and to furnish all possible aid to the "Bunker System" which the United States and Great Britain centered in the Caribbean to control routings of neutral vessels and thus prevent their employment in any fashion that might give aid to the Central Powers.

The numerous persons of Teutonic background resident in Panama who were suspected to be actual or potential agents of the Fatherland were arrested immediately after the declaration of war.[25] In many cases the arrests were actually made by United States officers accompanied by Panamanian police.[26] After a period of internment[27] they were all turned over to United States military authorities and removed to New York. Secretary of State Lansing assured the Panamanian government that the United States would save Panama harmless from any claims which might be pressed against her after the war for releasing these people to North American custody.[28] Secretary Lansing took the position that the two allied nations had a right to transfer "civilian internees" between their jurisdictions as an act in furtherance of their joint prosecution of the war, so long "as no changes in their legal status should occur."[29]

Through neutral intermediaries Germany bitterly protested the removal of these persons to New York as a gross violation of international law.[30] The United States obviously did not feel as confident of the legal grounds for its action as the assertions of Secretary Lansing would indicate. This is shown by the fact that after the cessation of hostilities all persons who had originally been arrested within the jurisdiction of Panama were returned to the Isthmus and released upon the soil of the Republic.[31] I have not been able to discover any instance of claims against the Republic of Panama being pressed successfully by any of the affected individuals.[32]

The "Bunker System," along with the "Black List," was a principal weapon of the Allied war effort in Latin America. Along with the three Venezuelan ports of La Guaira, Puerto Cabello, and Maracaibo, and Curacao in the Dutch West Indies, the Panama Canal ports were the bunker control stations. Licenses were required for all bunker fuel, sea or ships stores, and other supplies obtained at these ports. Inasmuch as vessels of virtually all of the Latin American countries regularly transited the Canal, or called at Colón or Balboa, it was habitual for them to take on fuel and stores there. An unequaled opportunity was thus given to the Allies to control sailing routes and schedules by issuing only enough fuel and stores to ships that they would be compelled to follow Allied routing instructions without deviation. This system was a powerful coercive to be applied particularly against those states of the hemisphere which persisted in remaining neutral or even on occasion had displayed pro-German sentiments.

The delays and inconveniences of this procedure were galling beyond description to a region whose only effective contact with the outside world was by sea. The United States enforced the bunker licenses with insidious effects. Ships of Chilean and Peruvian lines believed to be operating in German interests were widely diverted, and others were delayed by carefully calculated preferences given to friendly vessels.[33] It has been estimated that bunker license regulations operated to tie up and delay more shipping in Panama than all other defense measures combined.[34] Panama was constantly subjected to importuning pressures of all sorts, from within her sister Latin American states, to connive in schemes for circumventing the Bunker Regulations by allowing assistance to vessels in territorial waters adjacent to the Canal Zone, and at small ports such as Bocas del Toro in the province of the same name, and David, in Chiriqui. Sometimes these activities included the landing of clandestine passengers, escape of prohibited aliens in transit through the Canal Zone, and entry of unauthorized persons into restricted defense areas near the entrances of the Canal.[35] However, the Isthmian government was consistently loyal to its Allies in dealing with these matters.

A long series of agreements with the Canal Zone and U.S. military and naval authorities evinces the faithful coöperation of Panama in making Allied control measures effective. The beacon light at Toro Point was extinguished as a war measure to prevent strange vessels from approaching the coast,[36] the government censored newspapers to prevent advertising the arrival and departure of ships,[37] the U.S. authorities at Cristobal were allowed to screen all passengers departing from Colón and detain suspicious individuals.[38] Lieutenant William J. Burke, U.S. Army, was appointed a special quarantine officer at Bocas del Toro, which seemed to be an especially ticklish spot,[39] and a procedure for complete mail censorship on the Isthmus was worked out whereby Panamanian censors worked under North American supervision and were paid with U.S. funds.[40]

The "Black Lists" were lists of firms with which United States nationals and firms were forbidden to trade because of suspected connections with the Central Powers. They were sometimes called "Enemy Trading Lists" and were published at intervals three times during the war by the U.S. War Trade Board.[41] In addition to these three published lists there was also a "Confidential List" which contained names upon whom it was inexpedient to place a public ban or who could be effectively handled in private; and a "Confidential Cloaks List" which contained fictitious concerns used to mask enemy operations. These confidential lists were "For use of the Officials of Associated Governments only."[42]

As we have seen there were numerous Teutonic influences in Panamanian life. The list of October 6, 1917 contained ten Panamanian firms, the list of April 20, 1918 included thirteen, and the third and final list of December 13, 1918 held twenty-one. The Confidential List named two Panamanian concerns, and the Cloaks List also contained two Isthmian names.[43] There was much dissatisfaction in Latin America generally over these lists, and in Panama, because of its close economic ties with the United States, considerable financial loss was sustained by citizens of the Republic affected by the boycott, but the Panamanian government officially refrained from any protest or remonstrance and accepted this interdicting of its citizens and business concerns as a necessary sacrifice to the Allied cause.[44]

In fact the Government left no step untaken which could contribute to the Allied war effort by stamping out German activity upon the Isthmus. German properties and businesses were seized,[45] as well as German persons and their sympathizers. German and pro-German educators and students were removed,[46] and the press often fanned the flames of popular sympathy for the Allies.[47]

In October, 1918, the Republic of Panama officially gave its backing to the drive for the Fourth Liberty Loan. A monster parade was sponsored under joint Canal Zone-Panama auspices at both the Atlantic and Pacific terminal cities. This demonstration resulted in a subscription to the Liberty Loan in Panama City of $130,000 and in Colón of over $125,000, exclusive of Canal Zone contributions.[48]

A three-day holiday was proclaimed to celebrate the end of the war on November 11, 1918,[49] and amidst the rejoicing there was much approval of the post-war aims declared by President Wilson in his Fourteen Points address of some months before.[50] In retrospect the Republic of Panama had every right to feel that she had earned the seat, which would now be assigned to her, as one of the victorious belligerents, at the forthcoming Peace Conference at Versailles. She had taken every step required of her by the combination of Associated and Allied powers with which she had aligned herself, and shared with them the happy outcome, as it then seemed, of the greatest project in international collaboration which the world had known to that time.

Footnotes

CHAPTER FOUR

In the First World War

1. Gordon Ireland, *Boundaries, Possessions, and Conflicts in Central and North America and the Caribbean* (Cambridge, Mass., 1941), pp. 394-95.
2. Norman J. Padelford, *The Panama Canal in Peace and War* (New York, 1942), p. 124n.
3. *Ibid.*, p. 126.
4. Narciso Garay, *Panamá y las Guerras de los Estados Unidos* (Panamá, 1930), pp. 4-5. See also Victor F. Goytía, *La Función Geografica Del Istmo* (Panamá, 1947), p. 116.
5. Padelford, *supra*, p. 129n.
6. *Ibid.*, p. 129-30n.
7. The text of the Lansing-Morales Protocol appears in Garay, *Panamá y las Guerras de los Estados Unidos, supra*, p. 5. See also U.S. State Department, *Foreign Relations 1914, op. cit.*, pp. 984-85.
8. República de Panamá, Secretaría de Relaciones Exteriores, *Memoria 1916* (Panamá, 1919), p. 63.

9. U.S. War Department, *Annual Report of the Governor of the Canal Zone, 1918* (Washington, 1919), p. 137. See also the *Panama Canal Record,* Vol. 10 of 1916-17 (Ancon, Canal Zone, 1918), p. 489.

10. Padelford, *supra,* p. 130n.

11. U.S. State Department, *Decimal Files 862.20219/56 to 862.20221/13* (Box 9652), contains a complete documentation of pro-German activity in Panama during World War I.

12. Examples from U.S. State Department, *Decimal Files,* supra: Osterhout, Consul at Bocas del Toro to Minister Price, at Panama, November 20, 1917 reported the provincial governor and most local authorities pro-German; Price, at Panama, to Lansing, May 22, 1917 advised of activities of German Consul at Bocas del Toro, a Carl Friese; and Price to Lansing, May 21, 1917 reported that United Fruit Co. employees had uncovered a German supply base on the Sixaola River.

13. J. F. Normano, *The Struggle for South America* (Boston, 1931), pp. 77-81.

14. Berguido and Fabrega, *Manual etc., op. cit.,* p. 35. See also State Department, Dispatch No. 2228, Price to Lansing, of December 21, 1918.

15. República de Panamá, Secretaría de Relaciones Exteriores, *Memoria 1918-1920* (Panamá, 1921), pp. xxxviii-xxxix (1918 sec.), and pp. xxiii-xxiv (1920 sec.).

16. U.S. State Department, *Conf. Dispatch 1400,* Price, at Panama, to Lansing, May 24, 1917.

17. Quoting from a letter written by John Foster Dulles to Thomas A. Bailey and published in Bailey's *The Policy of the United States Toward the Neutrals, 1917-1918* (Baltimore, 1942), p. 27n.

18. República de Panamá, Secretaría de Relaciones Exteriores, *Documentos relacionados con la actual Guerra Europea* (Panama, 1918), pp. 12-13. See also Secretaría de Relaciones Exteriores, *Memoria 1918-1920, supra,* pp. iii-vi (1918 sec.).

19. U.S. State Department, *Foreign Relations, 1914 Supplement, op. cit.,* pp. 248-50.

20. U.S. State Department, Dispatch 3692 of April 6, 1917, Price, from Panama, to Lansing.

21. Garay, *Panamá y las Guerras de los Estados Unidos, supra,* pp. 49-54.

22. Interestingly enough it was feared that this might even allow bases to be created in nearby countries from which air attacks could be launched against the Canal. (State Department, Dispatch 1877, Price to Lansing, April 2, 1918). Also *Decimal File 20221/4,* Belden, at Bogotá, to Lansing, February 27, 1917, No. 362.

23. Garay, *supra,* p. 28.

24. Bailey, *Policy of the U.S. toward the Neutrals, 1917-1918*, *supra*, p. 316.

25. The legal position of Panama was explained in a typical case: Foreign Office Communication No. 610, Panamá, April 26, 1917: Narciso Garay, Ministro de R. E.–O. J. H. Schulz, "Prisoner of War": "I must inform you that owing to the state of war existing between Panama and Germany . . . the Government of Panama, acting in accord with that of the United States, decided, as a precautionary step, to intern certain German subjects located in our territory . . . in abnormal times such as the present international law justifies steps of this nature which are adopted through necessity, and with no desire to injure anyone." See Garay's own work, *Panamá y las Guerras de los Estados Unidos, supra*, pp. 73-90, for aspects of the Panamanian Constitutional guarantee of personal rights.

26. U.S. State Department, *Foreign Relations, 1918 Supplement*, Vol. II, pp. 232-33.

27. On beautiful Taboga Island—a source of sarcastic comment in the press—ex. "B.V.D." in *The Panama Morning Journal*, for September 16, 1917, saying "Gee but it's great to be a German, and get an expense paid vacation at Taboga!"

28. República de Panamá, Archivo Nacional, Secretaría de Relaciones Exteriores, No. 390 of June 21, 1917; Lansing to Garay: "This government will hold Panama harmless against loss on account of having interned persons in conformity with this government's desires."

29. U.S. State Department, *Foreign Relations, 1918 Supplement*, Vol. II, *supra*, pp. 234-35.

30. Panamá, Secretaría de Relaciones Exteriores, *Memoria 1918-1920, supra*, pp. xiii-xv. Also Archivo, Message 331 of December 6, 1917 from Luis San Simon y Ortega, Spanish Vice Consul in Panama handling German interests, to Garay. Germany threatened by way of reprisal to imprison five Panamanian students then at German universities. See also Panama *Star and Herald*, August 8, 1924.

31. U.S. State Department, Dispatch 2388 of May 29, 1919 from Panama. Also tel. rec'd. at 3 p.m., July 15, 1919 from Legation at Panama. Also U.S. War Department, *Report of the Governor of the Canal Zone, 1919* (Washington, 1919), p. 260.

32. One claim was pressed very hard, but disallowed. This was the claim of the wife of an interned alien for medical bills which her husband could not pay because of imprisonment. See State Department, *Decimal File 862.20219/207*, Lansing to Price, November 1, 1919.

33. *Report of the United States War Trade Board* (Washington, 1920), p. 59.

34. Padelford, *supra*, p. 150n.

35. U.S. War Department, *Annual Report of the Governor of the Canal Zone, 1918* (Washington, 1918), pp. 271-72. Also U.S. State Department, Dispatch No. 2154 from Panama, October 29, 1918, Price to Lansing.

36. U.S. War Department, *Annual Report of the Governor of the Canal Zone, 1917* (Washington, 1917), p. 271 (Appendix G).

37. U.S. State Department, Dispatch No. 2071 from Johnson, at Panama, to Lansing, August 27, 1918. See also U.S. War Department, *Report of the Governor of the Canal Zone, supra,* p. 270.

38. U.S. War Department, *Report of the Governor of the Canal Zone for 1919, supra*, p. 259.

39. *Ibid.,* p. 260. See also U.S. State Department, Dispatch 1684 from Price, at Panama, to Lansing, November 23, 1917.

40. Bailey, *Policy of the U.S. toward the Neutrals, supra,* p. 429. See also U.S. State Department, *Foreign Relations 1914, op. cit.*, pp. 1046-47, *and* for *1915*, p. 1123.

41. *Ibid.,* p. 362.

42. *Ibid.,* p. 360. See also U.S. State Department, Dispatches, all by telegraph, from Panama, August 28, 1918, unnumbered; 3 p.m., November 21, 1918; and 6 p.m., December 30, 1918.

43. Bailey, *Policy of the U.S. toward the Neutrals, supra,* p. 364.

44. See Garay, *Panamá y las Guerras de los Estados Unidos, supra*, "Comercio con el Enemego," pp. 65-70. See also U.S. State Department, Dispatch 2066, from Panama, August 29, 1918, containing the decrees of Panama giving effect to the blacklist and counter-espionage measures.

45. U.S. State Department, Dispatch 2169, from Panama, November 13, 1918, regarding seizure of German lands in Puerto Piñas owned by the "Balboa and Pacific Estates Co."

46. See Editorial "German Sentiment in Panama," *Panama Morning Journal*, September 30, 1918, in which the National Institute was attacked. See also U.S. State Department, Dispatch 2106, from Panama, September 30, 1918, concerning pro-German feelings in certain circles.

47. *Panama Morning Journal,* October 1, 1918.

48. U.S. Department of State, unnumbered Dispatch, Price, at Panama, to Lansing, October 12, 1918.

49. U.S. State Department, Dispatch, from Panama, rec'd. by telegraph, 8 p.m., November 13, 1918.

50. Editorials, *Panama Star and Herald,* November 12, 1918. See also U.S. State Department tel. dispatch from Panama, Price, to Lansing, October 29, 1918.

CHAPTER FIVE

Membership in the League of Nations

THE LEAGUE OF NATIONS had every reason to attract the states of Latin America. The new organization seemed to many Ibero-Americans to offer an ideal counterpoise to the "Colossus of the North." When the United States refused to enter the League the natural result was an acceleration of support for it among the nations to the south in the Western Hemisphere. J. Fred Rippy expresses the opinion that their adhesion to the League was even "caused in a measure by *fear* of the United States."[1]

This fond hope of some Hispanic Americans that the League would serve to balance North American power had particular application to Panama. The circumstances of the Revolution of 1903, the Hay-Bunau-Varilla Treaty, and subsequent *Yanqui* methods in administering the Canal Zone and in dealing with Panama had made that Republic a favorite text at the wailing walls of "Anti-Gringo" zealots, such as Manuel Ugarte,[2] throughout Latin America.

In 1919, 1920, and 1921, once the wartime collaboration was past, "anti-gringoism" reached a new high in Panama. Many traces of it are easily discernible. During the war there had been bitterness over excesses committed by servicemen on leave in Colón, over further expropriations of Panamanian territory for "defense" purposes under the terms of the Hay-Bunau-Varilla Treaty, and over some highhanded measures taken by the Canal Zone authorities regarding censorship, etc. During the visit of President-elect Harding to Panama in November, 1920, the local press had given vent to some of this spleen. The *Star and Herald* had this to say:

. . . in the last 8 years there have occurred painful events which have given rise to the complaint of the Panamanian people, that, even when not unheeded, received little satisfaction, leaving in the depths of the soul of Panama a measure of bitterness. . . .[3]

El Diario, another daily newspaper, commented:

. . . the visit which Mr. Harding is making may give him a conception of the various problems which exist in the complicated net of relations which, because of the Canal, we maintain with his people . . . mere wishes are not enough, nor patriotic utterances, nor even the refined fulfillments counselled by courtesy. It is necessary that there enter into play also serious considerations, especially of our own interests.[4]

The same paper said on January 15, 1921:

With regard now to the question of constant annexation of South American territory . . . under pretext of fortification of the Canal, we ask ourselves, what do Argentine, Chile, Peru, Ecuador, etc. think of this? A good portion of this part of Latin America will finally be occupied at this rate.[5]

United States diplomats in confidential messages to Washington made a gloomy appraisal of the state of mind of Panama's leading public figures. Such prominent men as Julio J. Fábrega, Eusebio A. Morales, and Santiago de la Guardia were found to be openly hostile,[6] and even Ricardo J. Alfaro, who in later years was often to prove himself a fast friend of the United States, was declared in 1922 to be definitely anti-American.[7] Minister William J.

Price summed up the subject of Panama and the League very clearly in a dispatch to Secretary of State Bainbridge Colby in January, 1921.

There exists the impression, perhaps a distinctly growing one, that Panama as one of the small countries will be distinctly benefited by its membership in the League of Nations, and that it will, at least eventually, be afforded a better opportunity to have settled questions that may arise with our government, such as the proper interpretation of the provisions of the Canal Treaty of 1903.[8]

During the 1920's various Panamanian regimes had to steer a cautious course between the powerful influences of the Harding-Coolidge administrations emanating from Washington, and the explosive force of domestic nationalism on the other hand. Generally it can be concluded that the interests favored by the North American government were best served in matters in which Panama, the League, and the United States were involved. But such results, though supporting the world position of the United States, were usually achieved at the price of bitter anti-*Yanqui* feeling among the people of Panama.

At the Versailles Peace Conference, where Panama was represented by Antonio Burgos,[9] the Republic's Minister to Spain, the Isthmian state was one of ten Latin American nations to become charter members of the new World Organization by subscribing to the Peace Treaty and the Covenant of the League of Nations. The experience of Panama at Versailles was of a somewhat embarrassing nature. Señor Burgos behaved in an erratic fashion. Not only did he liberally distribute "medals" and "decorations" not authorized by his government, but he stirred up a little tempest of indignation when he was accused of quoting the British statesman, Chamberlain, as having made remarks which in fact he had never uttered.[10] The government at Panama City took the lesson of this unfortunate incident to heart, and generally top-flight diplomats thereafter were sent to represent Panama in the League of Nations. Señor Burgos himself apparently profited from this incident, grew in diplomatic stature, and was much respected at Geneva when he later served there again as Panama's representative. The act of ratification of the Covenant by the National Assembly was deposited November 25, 1920, marking that as the official date of adherence to the League by Panama.[11]

Interest upon the Isthmus ran high as the first session of the Assembly of the League of Nations was held. In contrast with the choice of Antonio Burgos to go to Versailles, the Republic sent Harmodio Arias, a distinguished lawyer, and Narciso Garay, the wartime Minister of Foreign Affairs, to the League Assembly.[12] Dr. Arias served on the Commission of the International Court of Justice and attracted attention by sponsoring an amendment setting forth the principle of compulsory arbitration of the interpretation of treaties.[13] Narciso Garay made a speech before the Assembly supporting the move to have Spanish included as an official language of the League.[14]

At the First Assembly Panama joined other small nations in support of the French idea that real teeth should be incorporated into the system of Sanctions in order to enforce security for each state, as opposed to the British view that security could best be achieved by pushing for voluntary world-wide disarmament.[15]

The work of her delegation at the First Assembly, and particularly the acclaim received by Arias from quarters such as the *New York Herald*[16] occasioned much pride in Panama. The daily *Star and Herald* had this to say: "Dr. Arias' participation has been a positive honor to himself and to Panama, who can feel that one of her sons knew how to place her name high in an international body."[17]

Panama's attendance at the League Assembly remained constant and consistent through the early years of the League's existence.[18] Like some of her Latin American sisters she seemed to neglect the Pan American movement in her enthusiasm for the World Organization. Yet there never was any suggestion of liquidating either the Inter-American system or her part therein. Rather the trend seems to have been to work for a reorientation of the Inter-American system to a level of coöperation with the League and perhaps an ultimate role of subordination as a sort of regional agency of the World Organization.[19] Particularly in the early 1930's were strong efforts made to bring about practical coöperation between the two agencies in the 15th and 16th Assemblies.[20] By that time, however, the future of the League was appearing to be of much more doubtful quality, and there was little support in Latin America for an idea of bringing their regional organization into a position of subservience to the World body. Insofar as Panama was concerned the record of participation during the first ten years of the League's existence was a chapter of disappointment and frustration in the main.

Panama always had difficulty maintaining its financial standing in the League. It protested against the scale of contributions assessed to it at the outset, and at the Third Assembly the Republic's delegate, Dr. Amador, opposed an increase in the League budget.[21] At the Fifth Assembly Narciso Garay made a strenuous effort in the Fourth Committee to get Panama's quota lowered, but without success. The situation was later eased when Panama received a fair share of surplus funds, which were distributed to member states.[22]

One of the most involved problems affecting Latin America's relations within the League was the question of representation upon the Council. In lieu of giving any single Latin American state permanent representation upon this high body the arrangement was to give all American states (aside from the United States, which would have held a permanent seat) collectively three temporary seats which would rotate among the twenty Latin republics of the Western Hemisphere. This settlement had not been at all satisfactory to Brazil. She had conceived of herself as the logical "patron of American rights and interests" as the greatest power of the New World represented in the League after the default of the United States. Panama was placed in an embarrassing position by this controversy. She had an old tradition of friendship for Brazil.[23] At the Third Assembly Antonio Burgos, back in good graces and now one of Panama's delegates, had proposed that permanent members of the Council be elected by the Assembly.[24] This might have been a satisfactory compromise which would have enabled Brazil to be elected to permanent tenure, but nothing came of it. In 1926 Brazil sought to rally her hemispheric neighbors in support of her ambitions for the permanent seat, but many of them looked with a jaundiced eye on Brazil's pretensions and preferred to keep the arrangement of having three temporary seats always rotating among them. In the showdown no less than ten Latin American states voted against Brazil, and the great Amazonian republic quit the League in a huff.[25] Panama, however, was not among the ten.[26] Her traditional friendship with Brazil held firm. In general the Panamanian delegates supported regional claims as they were advanced in the Assembly. In the Third Session Señor Amador made a speech deploring the fact that the Secretariat had only one Latin American in its membership,[27] and in September 1923 Panama supported the move

MEMBERSHIP IN THE LEAGUE OF NATIONS 59

to establish a "Latin American Bureau" of the League.[28]

The most publicized matter involving Panama, the League, and the United States was the boundary dispute with Costa Rica which almost led to war between the two Central American republics in 1921. Volumes have been written covering all phases of this controversy,[29] and I shall repeat here only the salient features necessary to the continuity of the subject of Panama's role in the League of Nations.

Panama inherited this bitter dispute from the mother state—Colombia. An arbitration award handed down in 1900 by President Loubet of France gave Costa Rica a considerable amount of territory which had been claimed by Colombia—the Atlantic Coast of the Isthmus from Cape Mona to the San Juan River, and the Pacific Coast from the mouth of the Golfito River in Dulce Gulf to Burica Point. The government of Panama after 1903 concluded with Costa Rica a boundary treaty based upon the French award, but the act of ratification by the Panamanian Assembly read into the treaty definitions of boundaries which Costa Rica would not accept. Both republics agreed, in 1910, to accept U.S. mediation of the question of interpreting the Loubet Award. The Chief Justice of the United States Supreme Court, Edward Douglas White, was named Arbitrator.[30]

Justice White's decision was rendered in September 1914, after protracted and elaborate arguments by batteries of international law specialists. Panama refused to accept the White decision on the ground that he had "revised" rather than "interpreted" the Loubet Award. For several years there was a succession of acrimonious diplomatic interchanges, and in February 1921 a detachment of Costa Rican soldiers entered a village on the Coto River east of Golfito. A skirmish with Panamanian police ensued, and the "invaders" were taken prisoner. In March a second Costa Rican expedition met with the same fate.

When the news of this crisis reached the League offices the Secretary General, Sir Eric Drummond, wired at once for information. In reply the Panamanian government asked Drummond to inform the Council that Costa Rica had violated the national frontiers of the Isthmian Republic, and a request was made for application of sanctions against Costa Rica in accordance with the terms of the Covenant.[31] In the meantime President Harding had rather forcefully urged upon both countries the mediation of the United States.[32] Foreign Minister Alejandro Alvarado Quiros of Costa Rica seized upon this to saucily inform the League that the dispute was "virtually resolved" thanks to the intermediation of the United States.[33] With this the League, as J. Fred Rippy puts it, "beat an almost indecorous retreat."[34] Drummond "congratulated" both nations that their dispute was so amiably in the process of settlement.[35]

This tongue-in-check hypocrisy of the World Organization, as expressed in the foregoing message of the Secretary-General, left Panama displomatically stranded and at the charity of the United States. And the United States was not disposed to be charitable toward the Panamanian views, which snubbed the finding of the U.S. Arbitrator in 1914. The Harding Administration was adamant that Panama "fully comply with her international obligations,"[36] i.e., carry out the Loubet Award in accordance with the interpretation placed upon it by the North American Chief Justice White, to which Panama was bluntly reminded she had agreed in advance! When President Belisario Porras took the unusual step of asking President Harding to overrule Secretary of State Hughes, who

MEMBERSHIP IN THE LEAGUE OF NATIONS 61

had stated this position, he was summarily turned down, and it was announced that the U.S.S. *Pennsylvania* was sailing for Panama with a battalion of Marines to enforce settlement in accordance with the White judgment.[37]

Panama could do nothing in the face of such a threat, and on August 23, 1921, recalled her police and officials from the Pueblo Nuevo de Coto. Costa Rica occupied the area peacefully on September 5, 1921. Then diplomatic relations were broken off, and were not resumed until 1928 under the good offices of Chile.[38] In 1938 the Rodriguez-Garay Convention was signed at San José providing a settlement on the basis of Costa Rica conceding about 5,000 acres on the Atlantic coast north of the Sixaola River, and Panama giving up about 5,800 west of the same river, with the Loubet-White awards otherwise being observed. The Costa Rican Congress never acted upon this treaty and in October of 1938 President Arosemena of Panama denounced it. The boundary remained a de facto affair until 1944. In that year the Presidents of Panama and Costa Rica gave final approval to the 1938 agreement, ratifications were duly exchanged, and one of the sorest spots in Inter-American relations was finally eliminated.[39]

The fact that this controversy was quieted in 1921 by the overshadowing *Yanqui* colossus in a fashion so humiliating to Panama and to the League of Nations alike was a very severe blow to the prestige of the World Organization not only in Panama but in all Latin America. Their greatest fear was now given substance—the League would not be able to guarantee the long-dreamed-of "juridical equality of states" to protect the Latin nations of the Western Hemisphere against the military, economic, and political power of the United States. The utter collapse of Panama's confidence was expressed in these bitter words of Ricardo J. Alfaro: "Coerced and threatened by the greatest power in the world, Panama, defenseless, had to retire from the territory she had bravely defended."[40]

This affair even had repercussions in relation to another dispute in Latin America which was to add a new chapter to the ineffectuality of the League of Nations. The Panamanian populace remained agitated over the Costa Rica "settlement" for several years after 1921 because of continued discussion of the matter in the press, in books, and by public speakers. In 1925 the news that General Pershing and his mission were in Balboa en route to Tacna-Arica stirred the people of Panama City to riotous demonstrations against the United States—unmistakable reminders for Pershing that his country had problems still unsolved in Latin American relations much closer home than Tacna-Arica.[41]

The failure of the League of Nations to safeguard small states was watched with dismay by Latin America, but many of the lesser American powers continued to hope against hope that somehow, some way, the League would find a way to impose its will and effect a system of international security. In 1931 they battled valiantly along these lines when the Japanese invasion of Manchuria shook the World Organization to its very foundations. In December of that year during debate over the Manchurian affair in the Assembly Panama insisted upon the "inviolability of each state's territory," and "absolute non-intervention."[42] When the Lytton Commission made its report to the League and Japan was demonstrated to have made an entirely unwarranted and arrogant violation of China's integrity, the Panamanian delegates spoke in favor of taking sanctions against Japan.[43]

In 1926 Panama had been involved in another affair which resulted in a loss of prestige for the League of Nations. This was the abortive Kellogg-Alfaro Treaty.

Panama had long sought for revisions in the Hay-Bunau-Varilla Treaty of 1903 on the ground that it infringed the national sovereignty. The 1926 pact expressed changes which the United States was then willing to make. These were (1) an agreement to prohibit commercial establishments in the Zone other than those operated by the U.S. Government for its own employees, (2) a promise to restrict sales of the commissaries, and occupation of quarters, in the Canal Zone only to employees of the United States and their families, and (3) an agreement to give Panamanian merchants facilities for making sales to ships in Canal Zone waters.[44]

But the obligations which were to be assumed by Panama under the treaty aroused fierce opposition among the citizens of that Republic. They objected to a clause which would require Panama to participate in any war in which the United States should become involved, to requirements that Panama undertake an expensive program of road construction, to U.S. control of military operations on Panamanian soil, to further rights to expropriate Panamanian territory, and to the failure of the United States to completely end the competition between Canal Zone businesses (including even the commissaries) and enterprises within Panama. There was also unrest because the North Americans would do nothing to control the rampant smuggling of goods from the Canal Zone into the Republic.[45] Great popular demonstrations were staged in Colón and Panama City, and threats of death were hurled at members of the Assembly and government who dared to express any sentiments favorable to the treaty.[46]

The League of Nations thrust its head into this tense picture and created another opportunity for it to suffer a smashing "loss of face." The League officially expressed the view that the terms of the pact were in conflict with

Panama's obligations under Article XII of the Covenant to submit all disputes which might lead her into war to an inquiry or arbitration, and that she could not therefore promise in advance to automatically participate with the United States in armed conflict because she was obliged by the Covenant not to resort to war until three months after a decision had been reached by the League's board of inquiry or of an arbitration board.[47]

This action by the League was needless in view of the utter improbability of Panamanian ratification of the treaty. And yet, even after the National Assembly, on January 26, 1927, suspended all consideration of the draft treaty,[48] and thus had effectively killed the matter diplomatically, the League plunged blindly on to put the question on the agenda for the 8th Session of the General Assembly at Geneva on September 10, 1927.

Dr. Eusebio A. Morales, Finance Minister of Panama, took the floor at Geneva[49] ostensibly to explain that the proposed treaty was not a violation of the Covenant, and then opened the League to receive a humiliating rebuff by proposing from this world forum that the question of sovereignty over the Canal Zone be submitted to arbitration![50] In raising this issue Morales really touched upon one of the heaviest grievances of Panama. For her legal scholars had for years urged the point that the Republic had never given up sovereign ownership of the land included in the Canal Zone.[51] But the United States was not to be drawn into anything such as this, and two days after Morales spoke the U.S. State Department made a categorical announcement that between Panama and the United States there was *nothing* to arbitrate.[52] The "greatest power in the world" had thus served curt notice to the League that no influence whatsoever could interfere with its dealings with the Republic of Panama. This was a crushing blow to Panamanian hopes of finding in the League a refuge or protection against further *Yanqui* encroachments.

Although Panama certainly had as much reason as any Latin American state to lose faith utterly in the League of Nations she clung to membership in the face of every disappointment and defeat. In 1931 the Secretary-General, Sir Eric Drummond, paid a visit to Panama to attend, on January 19th of that year, a convocation in his honor of the *Sociedad Panameña de Derecho Internacional*.[53] At this time he was made an honorary member of the Society and in his address alluded to the high value and caliber of the services rendered to the League of Nations by Panama and her delegates over the years.[54]

Sir Eric particularly applauded the work of Narciso Garay, Harmodio Arias, and Octavio Méndez Pereira, but he might have mentioned many others as well. At the 1926 session Fabian Velarde had served as Alternate Secretary of the Assembly, and in 1931 Francisco Villalaz had been Secretary.[55] Raoul Amador would later have the distinguished honor of serving as President of the Council of the League of Nations during the LXXVII Session, October 4-26, 1933, and Belisario Porras would also later represent Panama on the Council.[56] Cristobal Rodriguez served on the staff of the International Labor Organization from 1923 to 1925,[57] and Horacio F. Alfaro and Octavio Méndez frequently distinguished themselves in their work as delegates to the League Assembly.[58]

As a member of the League Panama set a high example in international coöperation when, on January 14, 1929, she deposited her ratification of adherence to the International Court of Justice and was thus one of the few powers in the world to accept the principle of the compulsory jurisdiction of that body.[59] Being one of the smaller states and not always able to finance her delegations adequately Panama did not participate as actively in specialized agencies of the League as did some of the greater powers. She did attend the first and third conferences on Communications and Transit in 1921 and 1927, the Conference on Trade in Arms and Ammunitions in 1925, the International Economic Conference in 1927, and most of the conferences of the International Labor Organization, and of the Postal Union.[60] She also took an active role in the Latin American Liaison Bureau of the League and promoted its efforts to keep her sister nations of the hemisphere in the fold.[61] Cristobal Rodriguez served for years as secretary of this Bureau. This scholarly Panamanian was one of the most popular officials of the League's permanent staff. But in most of these particulars Panama was running against the trend.[62] When World War II put the final finishing touch to the League Panama was the only Central American state and one of the only six Latin American states to have stuck to the bitter end.[63]

Like a number of the members the small Isthmian Republic closed out her membership in arrears on her assessments, in default for the years 1925, and 1936-1945, to the amount of 104,000 Swiss francs.[64] The Board of Liquidation, set up when the League Assembly, at its 21st Ordinary Session on April 18, 1946, adopted the Final Article of Resolution for dissolution, decided to cancel Panama's arrears in assessments in recognition of her general record of loyal support.[65] Cynics may say that this was only a matter of face-saving on the part of the dying League, which could have no hope of collecting the assessments in any event. But there were a large number of other states beside Panama in arrears, and most of them were left listed in that category in the final report of the Board of Liquidations. Formal transfer of all assets of the League to the

United Nations was effected on August 1, 1946.⁶⁶ That date, presumably, should be taken as the official death date of the League of Nations. The Republic of Panama was with it to the last.

In summary it may be concluded, I think, that Panama's role in this great project of international coöperation served best to give color, in the instances of the Costa Rica boundary dispute and the Treaty of 1926, to the great need which Latin America had come to feel for such a World Organization as the League of Nations. Hispanic America sought in the League a Power that would acknowledge and guarantee the principle of the juridical equality of states. Panama contributed to the utmost every effort in her power to see this dream brought to reality. And when Latin America generally departed in disgust after it became clear that the League would be unable to accomplish such an end, the Republic of Panama was still willing to cling to the Society of Nations and to support it to the last in its fading hopes of preserving peace and right in the world.

Footnotes

CHAPTER FIVE

Membership in the League of Nations

1. J. Fred Rippy, *Latin America in World Politics* (New York, 1928), p. 238. See also the following articles: "Latin America after the War," *Living Age*, Vol. 23, pp. 14-19, July 2, 1921; "Latin America and the League of Nations," *Current History*, Vol. 28, pp. 181-84, May 1923, and "Latin America's Attitude toward the League of Nations," *ibid.*, Vol. 25, pp. 704-7, February 1923; and Stephen Duggan, "Latin America, the League and the United States," *Foreign Affairs*, Vol. 12, pp. 281-93, January 1934.

68   THE REPUBLIC OF PANAMA

2. Samuel F. Bemis, *The Latin American Policy of the U.S.*, *op. cit.*, p. 294. Also U.S. State Department, Dispatch 2168, from Panama, November 12, 1918, repeating contents of a letter from Angel Ugarte, there, to Manuel Ugarte, regarding conditions in Panama.
3. *Panama Star and Herald*, Panama City, November 26, 1920.
4. *El Diario Nacional*, Panamá, November 23, 1920.
5. *Ibid.*, January 15, 1921.
6. U.S. State Department, Dispatch 2728, from Panama, Price to Lansing, October 28, 1918.
7. U.S. State Department, *Decimal File 701.1911/172*, Minister South, at Panama, to Hughes, June 22, 1922.
8. U.S. State Department, *Decimal File 500C111/64*, Minister Price, at Panama, to Bainbridge Colby, January 10, 1921.
9. *Annuario de la Sociedad Panameña de Derecho Internacional, 1931-1933* (Panamá, 1933), p. 8. Also U.S. State Department, tel. dispatch, from Panama, rec'd. 9 a.m., January 20, 1919. In addition to Burgos, the delegation included Walker Penfield, Counsellor, and S. Heurtematteas, Secretary.
10. U.S. State Department, *Decimal File 701.1900*, Conf. Dispatch, Price, at Panama, to Hughes, May 28, 1921.
11. Denys P. Myers, ed., *Handbook of the League of Nations* (New York, 1935), p. 34.
12. U.S. State Department, *Decimal File 500C111/10*, Dispatch, Price to Colby, tel. rec'd. at 10 a.m., October 16, 1920.
13. *Star and Herald*, Panama, December 13, 1920.
14. *Star and Herald*, December 30, 1920.
15. Alfred Zimmern, *The League of Nations and the Rule of Law, 1918-1935* (London, 1936), p. 324.
16. *New York Herald*, November 28, 1920.
17. *Star and Herald*, Panama, December 27, 1920.
18. Warren H. Kelchner, *Latin American Relations with the League of Nations* (Boston, 1930), p. 120.
19. Victor A. Belaunde, "Latin America and the League," *Current History*, February, 1927, pp. 706 *et seq.*
20. League of Nations, *Official Journal, Special Supplement No. 125* (Geneva, 1934), p. 48n.; *Special Supplement No. 138* (Geneva, 1935), p. 127; *Special Supplement No. 139* (Geneva, 1935), pp. 63n, 93n. Also League of Nations Assembly, First Committee publ., *Relations between the League of Nations and the Pan American Union* (Geneva, 1935).
21. Warren H. Kelchner, *supra.*, p. 120.
22. *Ibid.*, p. 123.
23. See Chapter Two, p. 17, *supra.*

MEMBERSHIP IN THE LEAGUE OF NATIONS 69

24. Kelchner, *supra*, p. 122.
25. J. Fred Rippy, *Latin America in World Politics*, *supra*, pp. 240-41.
26. League of Nations, *Verbatim Reports of the Special Meeting of the Assembly*, March 1926 (Geneva, 1927), p. 29.
27. Kelchner, *supra*, p. 147.
28. *Ibid.*, p. 153.
29. The official attitudes of Panama and Costa Rica are presented in the following publications of the respective Ministries of Foreign Affairs: *Controversia de límites entre Panamá y Costa Rica; respuesta de Panamá a los Estados Unidos* (Panamá, 1921), 2 vol.; and *Documentos relativos al conflicto de jurisdicción territorial con la Republica de Panamá* (San José, 1921). For a private Panamanian view point: Ricardo J. Alfaro, *Costa Rica y Panamá, en defensa de los quieron Paz y Amistad* (Panamá, 1927). An excellent survey of the entire question in English: Gordon Ireland, *Boundaries, etc., op. cit.*, p. 33 *et seq.*
30. A complete record of the role of the U.S. in this controversy may be found in U.S. State Department, *Decimal File 718.1915/356*, at the National Archives, Washington, D. C.
31. League of Nations, *Official journal* (Geneva, 1921), pp. 214-19, 280, 341-44. Also State Department, *Decimal File 718. 1915/356*, Conf. Dispatch, Price, at Panama, to Hughes, rec'd. by tel., 12:09 a.m., March 11, 1921.
32. Gordon Ireland, *supra*, p. 39.
33. *Ibid.*
34. J. Fred Rippy, *Latin America in World Politics*, *supra*, p. 41.
35. *Official Journal of the League, supra*, p. 344.
36. U.S. State Department, *Foreign Relations 1921, op. cit.*, Vol. I, pp. 184-88.
37. *The Star and Herald*, Panama, March 20, 1921.
38. José Pozuelo A., *Por la Patria y por el amigo; testimonio relativo a los hechos que culminaron con el definitivo y feliz arreglo del problema fronterizo entre Costa Rica y Panamá* (San José, Costa Rica, 1943), 27 p.
39. República de Panamá, Ministerio de Relaciones Exteriores, *Memoria 1943-1944* (Panamá, 1945), p. xxii. The boundary treaty was signed, finally, at San José, May 1, 1944. Ratifications were exchanged September 18, 1944.
40. Ricardo J. Alfaro, *Costa Rica y Panamá, etc., op. cit.*, p. 10.
41. J. Fred Rippy, *supra*, pp. 256-57.
42. Margaret E. Burton, *The Assembly of the League of Nations* (Chicago, 1941), p. 309.
43. *Ibid.*, p. 322.

44. Raymond Leslie Buell, *Panama and the United States*, Foreign Policy Reports, Vol. VII, No. 23 (New York, 1932), p. 426.

45. República de Panamá, Secretaría de Relaciones Exteriores, *Memoria 1926* (Panamá, 1927), pp. xxiii-xl.

46. U.S. State Department, *Decimal File 711.192/284*, Conf. Dispatch, from Minister South, at Panama, to Kellogg, rec'd. by tel., 10 a.m., January 20, 1927.

47. *Official Journal of the League of Nations* (Geneva, 1927), pp. 100-103.

48. State Department, *Decimal File 711.192/284*, Conf. Dispatch from South, at Panama, to Kellogg, rec'd. by tel., 9 a.m., January 27, 1927.

49. State Department, *Decimal File 500.C111/289*, Conf. Dispatch from South, at Panama, to Kellogg, rec'd. by tel., 10 a.m., May 4, 1928.

50. State Department, Dispatch 1708 from Panama, May 19, 1928. Also Kelchner, *op. cit.*, p. 125.

51. Narciso Garay, *Panamá y las Guerras de los Estados Unidos, op. cit.*, pp. 110-43, discusses this point with relation to the 1926 Treaty. See also Victor F. Goytía, *Bases y Doctrinas de Derecho Publico*, 2 vols. (Panamá, 1948), containing numerous references to the juridical neutrality of the Isthmus; and by the same author, *La Función Geografica del Istmo* (Panamá, 1947), Chap. VIII, p. 113 *et seq.;* Francesco Cosentini, *Los Tratados y Las Convenciones de la Zona del Canal de Panamá . . . Las Bases Equitativas de un Nuevo Tratado* (Panamá, 1928); and the official Memoria of the Ministry of Foreign Affairs, *Documentos importantes relacionades con las negociaciones del tratado de 28 de julio de 1926 tomados de la Memoria de relaciones exteriores presentada a la Asamblea Nacional* (Panamá, 1927).

52. *New York Times* for September 13, 1927.

53. U.S. State Department, Dispatch 330, of January 24, 1931, from Davis, at Panama, to Stimson.

54. *Annuario de la Sociedad Panameña de Derecho Internacional, 1931-1933* (Panamá, 1933), p. 13.

55. *Ibid.*, p. 7.

56. Panama's representation on the Council during her term as a temporary or term member (1931-34) were Narciso Garay, LXV Session (Sept. 19-30, 1931) through the LXX Session (Jan. 24-Feb. 20, 1933); Raoul Amador, LXXI Session Extr. (Feb. 21-March 18, 1933) through the LXXVIII Session (Jan. 15-20, 1934); and Belisario Porras, from the LXXIX Session (May 14-19, 1934) through the LXXXI Session (Sept. 7-15, 1934). See Georges Ottlik,

ed., *Annuaire de la Société des Nations, 1936* (Geneva, 1936), pp. 1008-12, 1012-15, and 1016-17.

57. Kelchner, *Latin American Relations with the League of Nations, op. cit.,* p. 152.

58. U.S. State Department, Dispatch 138, of August 4, 1930, from Davis, at Panama, to Stimson; also Dispatch 668, of August 29, 1931, from Davis to Stimson.

59. *United Nations Yearbook, 1945-1946* (New York, 1947), p. 611.

60. Kelchner, *supra,* p. 140.

61. *Ibid.,* p. 153.

62. But without confidence. The evolution of the attitude of Panamanian statesmen from the high hopes of early days to the ultimate sense of disappointment in the League's "failure" may be seen in Ricardo J. Alfaro's "An American League of Nations," *World Affairs Magazine,* September 1938, pp. 137, 158 *et. seq.,* and in the same author's *Commentary on Pan American Problems* (Cambridge, Mass., 1938), p. 87.

63. League of *Nations, Final Report of the Board of Liquidation of the Assets of the League* (Geneva, 1947), p. 14.

64. *Ibid.,* p.30.

65. *Ibid.,* p. 30.

66. *Ibid.,* p. 16.

CHAPTER SIX

The Inter-American System, 1923-1938

WORLD WAR I had interrupted the progress and development of the Inter-American System. During the period between the Buenos Aires Conference of 1910 and the Fifth International Congress of American States at Santiago de Chile in 1923 there had been some fifteen odd meetings of Pan American agencies, as recounted in Chapter Three, but the top level congresses normally held every five years had been put aside before the pressing world problems of peace and war which occupied this thirteen-year span. During the war years the opening of the Panama Canal had been the principal event underlining Panama's future role in the Inter-American System, and that ceremony had been appropriately marked by John Barrett, Director General, and the Governing Board of the Pan American Union, in accordance with a resolution which the Buenos Aires Conference had adopted.[1] It had also been celebrated by the President of Panama, Belisario Porras, by most of his fellow citizens, and by representatives of nearly all of the nations of the civilized world.[2]

After the First World War, in the era which Professor Bemis has called the period of "The Republican Restoration,"[3] the U.S. Secretary of State, Charles Evans Hughes, was one who labored earnestly to remove some of the accumulated causes for Latin American ill will toward his country, and, as has been noted, his work in connection with the ratification of the Thomson-Urrutia Convention was of considerable importance to Panama.[4] However, the efforts of men like Hughes were often undone by the revived "Dollar Diplomacy" and "Big Stick" policies of the Harding and Coolidge Administrations.[5] There was no spot in Latin America where animosity toward the United States was more evident than in Panama during these years. The press spoke of ". . . the constant tyranny of relations between us and the United States due to the belief of the latter that they have the right to gradually eliminate our republic. . . ."[6] In 1922 when Ricardo J. Alfaro was appointed Minister to Washington, the U.S. Minister at Panama, John Glover South, filed a confidential dispatch appraising Alfaro as definitely "anti-American."[7] Nothing could better illustrate the low ebb of United States relations with Panama because just a few years before another U.S. diplomat on the Isthmus, William J. Price, had found Alfaro to be an outstanding and loyal friend of the United States.[8] The policies of the Harding Administration had proved too much to bear even among those who had long tried to be friends of the *Yanqui* colossus.

At the Fifth International Conference of American States in Santiago de Chile in 1923 feeling against the United States was higher among the Latin delegates than in any previous such meeting, and even the concept of Pan Americanism itself was beginning to be held in low esteem by many because of their despair that the United States could ever be persuaded to change its methods and viewpoints in hemispheric matters.

This conference broke down the traditional exclusion of political issues from the agendas of Inter-American Congresses, and Panama joined with her Latin sisters in overriding U.S. efforts to adhere to the old principle. Social questions, an attempt to limit naval armaments, Baltasar Brum's plan for an American League of Nations, and reorganization of the policy determining makeup of the Governing Board all came before this session.[9] On May 23, 1928, Panama deposited its ratification of the Conference's greatest accomplishment—the Gondra Treaty providing for permanent Inter-American machinery for settlement of disputes between nations of the hemisphere.[10]

Narciso Garay served as Vice-President of the Santiago Conference. José E. Lefevre was Panama's only other delegate.[11] Matters of particular interest to the Isthmian Republic were adoption of three resolutions extending the coöperation of the American states to the new Gorgas Institute,[12] to a celebration planned to honor Vasco Núñez de Balboa who had once dreamed of a transoceanic canal,[13] and to the Bolivarian Congress projected for Panama City in 1926.

During the month of April, 1926, the City of Panama proudly played host to the Pan American Congress in Commemoration of the Liberator, Simón Bolívar.[14] A statue of the Liberator erected as a gift from the Pan American Union was formally unveiled at these ceremonies. In conjunction with this celebration the sessions of the Pan American Congress of Women were also held in Panama City, and the Panamanian delegate, Señora Ester Neira de Calvo, played a very prominent role in this meeting.[15]

The practice of holding a top level, full-dress Pan American Conference every five years had been resumed with the Santiago meeting. The year 1928 therefore was the time of the next regular, or Sixth, International Conference of American States. Frank B. Kellogg was now

THE INTER-AMERICAN SYSTEM, 1923-1938 75

the United States Secretary of State. He had been a delegate at the Santiago Conference and, according to Sumner Welles,[16] the acrimonious relations between the United States and Latin America which had characterized many sessions of the 1923 conference had colored his outlook and had builded a climate of feeling in his mind distinctly hostile toward the Latin American nations. Together with President Coolidge's singular viewpoint that the United States could afford to snub and by-pass "insignificant peoples," this made for an electric atmosphere when the Sixth Conference assembled in 1928 at Havana, Cuba.

Panamanian opinion toward the United States in 1928 was then still seething over the abortive treaty of 1926, and the recent intervention of the U.S. Marines in nearby Nicaragua had heightened this animosity. It is generally considered that the Havana Congress represented the very ebb tide of Pan Americanism.

The distinguished Panamanian statesman, Ricardo J. Alfaro, served as Vice-President and Reporter on Arbitration at the Havana Conference, and Eduardo Chiari was the other delegate from Panama.[17] The Isthmian Republic was prepared to go along on Latin American proposals aimed to bring the *Yanqui* colossus to the bar of censure.[18] The report of the Commission of Jurists, which had been drafted at Rio de Janeiro a year before, was to be presented and it banned intervention of one state in the internal affairs of another. If adopted it would have thus indirectly condemned the incursion of the North American marines into Nicaragua.[19]

The United States battled to turn aside this threat by attempting to once again limit the agenda to traditionally nonpolitical spheres of discussion, and by passing out hints that great concessions in the field of arbitration might be forthcoming if her wishes in this matter were respected.

Victor Andres Belaunde says that although the Nicaraguan intervention overshadowed the Havana meeting the Latin delegates began to show a surprisingly "cautious and timid" attitude as the North American pressures began to tell.[20]

Ricardo J. Alfaro of Panama was not one of the timid souls. When President Coolidge addressed the Conference Señor Alfaro was cynical about his declaration upholding the sovereignty of small nations and endorsing stronger methods to guarantee it. He considered that the acts of the Coolidge Administration in applying a doctrine of unlimited protection of U.S. citizens abroad belied these fair words. To a Panamanian this policy seemed especially obnoxious because it was apparently intended for use only in Caribbean countries and not against the stronger nations.[21]

The Latin American front at Havana was not a solid one, and the United States did find allies in Peru, Cuba, and Nicaragua[22] in preventing the acceptance of the proposal to codify an American system of international law which would have scrapped the justifications for intervention traditionally held under European and general international law (viz. the Porter Proposition). However, Panama was not in the *Yanqui* "vest pocket" in this struggle. The sidetracking of the report of the Commission of Jurists was helped along by the inspired hints about forthcoming concessions in arbitration from the United States, and the proposal to call a special conference on arbitration to meet within the next year at Washington, D. C., to study the subject and propose machinery for conducting Inter-American arbitration.[23]

Panama was vitally concerned at Havana with a proposed Civil Aviation Convention, and an amendment offered by Henry Fletcher, for the United States, that any two signers of the Convention be authorized to exclude a third power's planes from their territories. It was feared that this constituted a subtle move to give Pan American Airways a monopoly in the Canal Zone.[24] The question was referred to a subcommittee of Fletcher and Olaya of Colombia. As finally passed the American proposal was modified to guarantee terminal facilities and equal treatment for commercial planes of all powers.[25]

A Convention and Code on Private International Law was also adopted by the Havana Conference. This was officially named the Bustamente Code.[26] The Panamanian delegation had originally expressed an intention to enter reservations to the portion covering application of national law to foreigners residing in the country.[27] When Article 7 was phrased to authorize every state to apply its own laws to foreigners Panama gave its approval without reservation.[28] The Republic ratified the convention on November 26, 1928.[29]

The meeting at Washington, D. C., in January 1929 on arbitration, which the Havana Conference had urged, drew up two treaties: a general treaty of international arbitration covering Inter-American disputes of a juridical character; and a Treaty of International American Conciliation, whereby the contracting parties agreed to submit to the consideration of commissions of inquiry established by the Santiago Conference certain existing controversies which had up to then defied solution by normal diplomatic procedures. These treaties were improvements upon the Gondra Treaty in that they set up real commissions of conciliation rather than mere fact-finding bodies.[30] Ricardo J. Alfaro, who represented Panama at Washington along with Carlos L. López,[31] declared that the treaties were the most advanced steps ever taken toward international peace and justice.[32] Panama signed both conventions on January

5, 1929, and deposited ratification of the former on January 20, 1933, and the latter on February 20, 1933.[33]

The spirit of the Briand-Kellogg Peace Pact (to which Panama adhered on December 19, 1928)[34] spilled over into the Inter-American System. Carlos Saavedra Lamas of Argentina sponsored an American anti-war pact which was signed at Rio de Janeiro October 10, 1933, by Panama, among others, and which provided for a commission of five to solve "conflicts or differences of whatever class," condemned wars of aggression, and pledged signatories not to recognize territorial adjustments produced by the use of force.[35] At the Seventh International Conference of American States at Montevideo in 1933 Panama supported a blanket resolution affirming the faith of the American states in five peace instruments—the Gondra Treaty, the Briand-Kellogg Pact, the Washington Arbitration and Conciliation Conventions of 1929, and the Saavedra Lamas Treaty above mentioned.[36]

The year 1933 brought the inauguration of Franklin D. Roosevelt as President of the United States. The high watermark of Panamanian bitterness toward the *Yanqui* colossus had probably been reached at the time of the 1926 Treaty and had receded slowly through the Hoover Administration as such measures as the Clark Memorandum (which abrogated the Roosevelt Corollary) gave new hope to the exponents of Pan Americanism.

This hope developed very slowly in Panama, and was only cautiously expressed. In 1931 the birthday of President Hoover was marked by friendly demonstrations in Panamanian schools,[37] and the publication of the Hoover Debt Moratorium in the same year[38] gave some impetus to the feeling that the Quaker North American President had injected more benevolence into United States foreign policy. The Clark Memorandum, despite its obviously very important implications for Panama, was received with only lukewarm applause in the Isthmian press. The United States Chargé d'Affairs, Benjamin Muse, reported to the State Department from Panama City:

The announcement . . . was given moderate publicity, and cabled dispatches were published reporting statements on the subject by Latin American diplomats in Washington, Buenos Aires, and Mexico. Such items were presented in generally friendly manner. No comments were made however by the Panamanian newspapers themselves in editorials or special articles.[39]

In view of past history Panama could scarcely avoid a certain skepticism about apparent changes in North American viewpoints. In 1930 the Republic's Minister of Foreign Affairs still felt constrained to make a public pronouncement that Panama would resist any further United States attempts to expropriate lands under the guise of requiring them for defense of the Canal if the Isthmian government were not able to see the existence of such a need.[40]

Because of the fact that the Isthmian state was so deeply involved with the United States the effects of the Good Neighbor policy were perhaps more far-reaching in Panama than anywhere else. The slow drift of the Roosevelt Administration toward acceptance of the long-dreamed-of doctrine of *absolute nonintervention* was watched with almost bated breath in Panama. At the Seventh Conference of the American States in Montevideo in 1933 the Panamanian delegates, J. D. Arosemena, Eduardo E. Holguín, Oscar R. Muller, and Magín Pons,[41] shared the disappointment of many other Hispanic American statesmen when Secretary Hull's acceptance of nonintervention was qualified by a reservation of North American treaty rights of intervention. The broad concessions of the Hay-Bunau-Varilla Treaty of 1903 in this respect meant that Panama's outlook was little changed by the position taken by the United States at Montevideo. For Panama *"El Peligro Yanqui"* was still a contingency which would depend upon the caprice of future regimes in Washington.

The Republic of Panama found its fondest hopes come to fruition in 1936. In that year the United States, represented by President Roosevelt in person, went to the special Inter-American Conference at Buenos Aires and finally gave full acceptance to the doctrine of absolute nonintervention. At the Buenos Aires meeting Harmodio Arias served as Vice-President of the Conference, and as President of the Fourth Committee (Juridical Problems). Other Panamanian delegates were Julio J. Fábrega and Eduardo Chiari.[42] Panama sponsored a proposal for an American Court of International Justice at this conference. A resolution for the study of the Panamanian project, and others on the same subject, was adopted, with the Juridical Committee to make a report on the study at the next regular Inter-American Conference in Lima.[43] The Buenos Aires meeting also provided that the Society of American Friendship, an association of a social and cultural character, be set up with headquarters in Panama City under the direction of Dr. Harmodio Arias.[44]

Panama was already assured of President Roosevelt's good faith in the Buenos Aires pronouncement. Earlier in 1936 the Hull-Alfaro Treaty had been negotiated,[45] and since it involved a surrender of treaty rights to intervene in Panama, held by the United States since 1903, it was a full expression of the new North American policy.

Panamanians for thirty years had chafed under the restrictive terms of the Hay-Bunau-Varilla Treaty. The well-known Isthmian writer, Ernesto de J. Castillero Reyes, had expressed the view of virtually all of his countrymen in terming it a "strangling noose" about the neck of the sovereign Republic of Panama.[46]

The Hull-Alfaro Treaty included not only the U.S. right of intervention going by the board, but also a surrender of the unilateral privilege, likewise possessed under the Hay-Bunau-Varilla Treaty,[47] of seizing additional Panamanian territory for the "operation and/or defense of the Canal." This last concession caused the United States Senate to hold up ratification of the pact until July 1939, when a provision for use of further Panamanian territory on a basis of "mutual understanding" was included.[48] As Sumner Welles, the North American negotiator, put it, Panama now became a partner rather than a subordinate of the United States in the protection of the great canal.[49] A long series of supplementary agreements on economic matters also did much to create a new climate of opinion toward *Yanquis* in Panama. Dr. Alfaro himself had this to say of the negotiations: "The treaty was made possible chiefly by the ability, the sense of justice, and the conciliatory spirit of . . . Mr. Sumner Welles, in whom the policy of the Good Neighbor has a most faithful interpreter."[50]

Outside the realms of diplomacy and international law the Republic of Panama has given its coöperation to numerous projects affiliated with the Pan American movement and its specialized agencies. Panama City has often played host to meetings of such groups prior to the Second World War era, including the Fourth Pan American Medical Congress in 1905, the International Sanitary Conference in 1924, the Bolivarian Commemoration Congress of 1926, the Inter-American Congress of Women held at the same time, the first Inter-American Highway Conference in 1929, the Second Congress of the Pan American Medical Association in 1930, and the Fourth Inter-American Postal

Congress in 1936 at which Canada and Spain were also represented. Panama City is the headquarters of the International (Postal) Transfer Office, and of the Inter-American University, which are agencies of the hemispheric organization.[51]

Panama has participated in virtually every one of the affiliated activities of the Inter-American System—the Scientific Congresses beginning in 1908 at Santiago; the International Sanitary Conferences after the Fourth in 1909 at San José; the Financial Conferences starting in 1915 at Washington; Child Welfare, 1919, at Montevideo; Red Cross, 1923, at Buenos Aires; Journalists, 1926, at Washington; Aviation, 1927, at Washington; Homoculture and Eugenics, 1927, at Havana; Trade Marks, 1929, at Washington; the Institute of Geography and History, 1929, at Mexico City; the Commission of Women, 1926, at Panama; the Congress of Rectors, Deans, and Educators, Havana in 1930; Agriculture, Forestry, and Animal Industry, Washington in 1930; and the Conference on Regulation of Automotive Traffic, also in Washington in 1930.[52]

Although the Inter-American Radio Conference was not formally organized until 1937 at Havana, Panama in 1930 accepted an international code covering long distance radio messages of a restricted character, and a radio telephone circuit was in operation between Panama and New York City, Cuba, Costa Rica, Colombia, Venezuela, Brazil, Argentina, and Chile. The Republic was very concerned with the conferences on aviation, and collaborated with the United States before the war to make Albrook Field at Balboa, and its approaches, a key airport in the Pan American network. The Pan American Conferences on Highways and the projected Pan American Highway, and the Conference on Regulation of Automotive Traffic were of a great importance to a nation whose jungle terrain loomed as a major obstacle to completion of the great international highway, but which as far back as 1930 boasted that in its capital city there was one automobile for every fifteen people; a very high average in Latin America.[53]

Some of Panama's citizens are particularly well remembered in connection with Pan American activities—Juan Antonio Susto in geography and history; Narciso Garay, Victor F. Goytía, Ramón M. Valdés, Harmodio Arias, and Ricardo J. Alfaro in American international law; Harris F. Bunker, Guillermo Andreve[54] and Jesús Vázquez Gayoso in education and cultural projects; Harmodio Arias in publishing; Señora Clara González in women's activities;[55] and Juan B. Chevalier in economic matters.[56] At the Fourth Pan American Commercial Conference in Washington in 1931 the Panamanian delegates, L. C. Aleman and Ramon Benedetti, created something of a stir by bringing up the old burning issue of the government-operated commissaries in the Canal Zone and their detrimental effects upon Panamanian commerce and trade.[57]

We have seen how the rapidly diminishing prestige of the League of Nations, coinciding with the expanding Good Neighbor policy of the United States, gave the Pan American movement a new life and importance. The developing era of good feeling seemed to have reached its climax at Buenos Aires in 1936 when the United States accepted in full the long cherished Doctrine of Absolute Nonintervention. For Panama the cup was nearly full when the Hull-Alfaro Treaty was negotiated setting forth that the United States was so wholeheartedly accepting the absolute concept of nonintervention as to surrender rights possessed for years under the solemn covenants of treaty obligations.

The new spirit of the Inter-American System came not

a day too soon. The threat implied in the unfolding program of Nazi Germany was casting its shadow even before the Buenos Aires meeting. But the brazen liquidation of Austria in 1938, events in the Far East the year before, and the Spanish Civil War, meant that the next meeting of the American States at Lima would have to face the acceleration of the Fascist menace to the entire World. Continental solidarity in the face of such a threat would appear to be a natural safeguard for small states in an age which imperiled the security of small states everywhere. Panama, the "Crossroads of the World," once again would inevitably be vitally concerned in the drift of that world toward the second global conflict of the twentieth century. As in 1914-1918, she would respond to the duty of coöperating with sister states of the hemisphere for the common security.

Footnotes

CHAPTER SIX

The Inter-American System, 1923-1938

1. James B. Scott, ed., *The International Conferences of American States, op. cit.,* p. 170.
2. Panama Canal Department, *Canal Record* (Ancon, C. Z.), Vol. VII, 521, August 19, 1914.
3. Samuel F. Bemis, *The Latin American Policy of the United States, op. cit.,* p. 202.
4. See Chapter Three, pp. 34-35, *supra.*
5. Bemis, *supra,* pp. 202-21.
6. *El Diario Nacional, Panamá,* January 14, 1921.
7. U.S. State Department, *Decimal File 701.1911/172,* Conf. Dispatch, South, at Panama, to Hughes, June 22, 1922.
8. U.S. State Department, Dispatch 2728, from Price, at Panama, to Lansing, October 28, 1918.
9. U.S. State Department, *Report of the Delegates of the United*

States to the Fifth International Conference of American States (Washington, 1924), pp. 3-8.

10. Gordon Ireland, *Boundaries, Possessions, and Conflicts, op. cit.*, p. 397.

11. U.S. State Department, *Decimal File 710.E002/S9*, Dispatch from South, at Panama, to Hughes, February 17, 1923.

12. J. B. Scott, ed., *Conferences, supra*, p. 242.

13. *Ibid.*, p. 282.

14. Ricardo J. Alfaro, *Panorama Internacional de America*, (Cambridge, Mass., 1938), p. 78.

15. U.S. State Department, Dispatch No. 1010, from South, at Panama, to Kellogg, April 20, 1926.

16. Sumner Welles, *The Time for Decision* (New York, 1944), p. 187.

17. Victor A. Belaunde, *The Havana and Washington Conferences* (in Quincy Wright, ed., *Interpretations of American Foreign Policy, op. cit.*), p. 153. See also Scott, ed., *supra*, p. 305.

18. U.S. State Department, *Decimal File 710.F002/50*, Dispatch from Martin, at Panama, to Kellogg, November 10, 1927, discusses generally the Panamanian attitude toward the forthcoming Conference.

19. Belaunde, *supra*, p. 144.

20. *Ibid.*

21. T. H. Reynolds, ed., *The Progress of Pan Americanism*, (Washington, 1942), p. 126.

22. John P. Humphrey, *The Inter-American System. A Canadian View* (Toronto, 1942), p. 126.

23. Belaunde, *supra*, p. 144.

24. Scott, ed., *International Conferences, supra*, p. 391.

25. Burr, *Colombia and International Cooperation, op. cit.*, pp. 160, 171.

26. República de Panamá, *Gaceta Oficial*, January 19, 1929.

27. U.S. State Department, Dispatches 1890, 1891, from South, at Panama, December 20, 1928.

28. República de Panamá, Asamblea Nacional, *Leyes aprobatorias de las convenciones suscritas en la sexta conferencia panaméricana celebrada en la Habana y de tratados y convenciones entre la república de Panamá y otras naciones. Edición oficial autorized por la Asamblea Nacional de Panamá* (Panamá, 1929).

29. Edward Schuster, *Guide to Law and Legal Literature of the Central American Republics* (New York, 1937), p. 117.

30. Belaunde, *supra*, p. 151.

31. J. B. Scott, ed., *International Conferences, supra*, p. 463.

32. Belaunde, *Havana and Washington Conferences, supra,* p. 153.
33. Ireland, *Boundaries, Possessions,* etc., *op. cit.,* pp. 398-400.
34. *Ibid.,* p. 398.
35. *Ibid.,* p. 400-401.
36. *Ibid.,* p. 401. The Montevideo Conference also adopted conventions on nationality of women, on extradition, and on naturalization. See Juan Antonio Susto, *Compilación, Indices, y Notas: Leyes Expedidas por la Asamblea Nacional, 1938* (Panamá, 1939), pp. 21, 29, 40.
37. U.S. State Department, Dispatch telegram 113, August 7, 1931, from Davis, at Panama, to Stimson.
38. U.S. State Department, Dispatch 636, August 7, 1931, from Davis to Stimson.
39. U.S. State Department, Dispatch 4017, of March 13, 1930, from Muse, at Panama, to Stimson.
40. República de Panamá, Secretaría de Relaciones Exteriores, *Memoria 1930,* Anexos I, p. xxii.
41. George A. Finch, ed., *Supplement to the International Conferences of American States, 1933-1940* (Washington, 1940), p. 14.
42. *Ibid.,* p. 138. See also Juan Antonio Susto, *supra,* p. 52.
43. Finch, *supra,* p. 144n.
44. *Ibid.,* p. 163. Besides the Additional Protocol relating to non-intervention, the Buenos Aires conference adopted various conventions to strengthen the Inter-American peace machinery and to further cultural relations. For action of the Panamanian Assembly in ratification of these see Juan Antonio Susto, *supra,* pp. 51, 60, 65, 70, 76, 81, 85, 91, 97, 103, and 109.
45. Asamblea Nacional, *Leyes expedidas por la Asamblea Nacional, 1936-1937* (Panamá, 1937); also, Secretaría de Relaciones Exteriores, *Memoria 1936 a 1937* (Panamá, 1938), Vol. XI, p. 51.
46. Ernesto J. Castillero R., *El Profeta Panamá y su gran traición: el tratado del Canal y la intervención de Bunau-Varilla en su confección* (Panamá, 1936), p. 57.
47. On this point see Publio A. Vásquez Hernandez, "La Personalidad internacional de Panamá," in *Boletín de la Academia Panameña de la Historia,* Ano I (Panamá, 1933), p. 587.
48. U.S. Congressional Record (76th Congress, First Session, 1939), pp. 9824-46; 9899-907.
49. Sumner Welles, *The Time for Decision, op. cit.,* p. 202.
50. Address by Ricardo J. Alfaro reprinted in T. H. Reynolds, *The Progress of Pan Americanism, op. cit.,* p. 133.

THE INTER-AMERICAN SYSTEM, 1923-1938 87

51. Warren Kelchner, ed., *Inter-American Conferences, 1826-1933, Chronological and Classified Lists* (Washington, 1933). See also Finch, ed., *Supplement to International Conferences of American States, supra,* pp. 405, 408, 433, 443, and 452.

52. Kelchner, *Chronological and Classified Lists, supra.* In connection with Panama's commitments to various inter-American economic, social, and political conventions attention is invited to the compilation in Edward Schuster, *Guide to the Law and Legal Literature of Central American Republics, op. cit.,* Chap. VI, pp. 99-118.

53. Guillermo Colunge, *The Republic of Panama, op. cit.,* p. 50.

54. J. B. Scott, ed., *The Inter-American Conferences, etc., op. cit.,* p. 487.

55. *Ibid.,* p. 495. Particularly as a member of the Inter-American Commission of Women and as Panama's delegate to the Conference of Women at Havana, February 17-24, 1930.

56. *Ibid.,* p. 482. Señor Chevalier was Panama's delegate to the Pan American Trade Mark Congress in Washington, February 1929.

57. U.S. State Department, Dispatch 685, of September 11, 1931, from Roy T. Davis, at Panama, to Stimson.

CHAPTER SEVEN

The Hemisphere Faces the Axis Threat

As the 1930's drew to a close, rumors of an impending general conflict in Europe and Asia had had substantial confirmation in the Italo-Ethiopian War, the march into the Rhineland, the Austrian Anschluss, and the Manchurian "incident." In the face of these events the United States inspired the Buenos Aires meeting of 1936, which was appropriately called "The Inter-American Conference for the Maintenance of Peace."[1]

This conference at Buenos Aires was eventful, as we have seen, for the United States' acceptance of the principle of absolute nonintervention for the Americas.[2] It also introduced the principle of mutual consultation among the American states, not only for the purpose of maintaining peace in this hemisphere but also for formulating effective Inter-American machinery for meeting any threat of aggression from abroad.[3] The Collective Security Pact, whereby the twenty-one republics resolved to consult upon methods to be adopted if a breach of the American peace should be threatened, was signed by Panama on December 23, 1936, and her ratification was deposited on December 7, 1938. Two companion treaties of the same date, setting up a board of mediators, and a permanent bilateral mixed commission to stave off controversial disputes, were ratified by the Republic on December 13,

1938.[4] The Protocol of Buenos Aires Relative to Non-Intervention stipulated that interference in the affairs of an American nation should be deemed a sufficient menace to set the new protective mechanism into operation.[5]

The great omission of the Buenos Aires Conference was the failure to provide machinery necessary for Inter-American consultation by specifically declaring that the heads of the respective departments of foreign relations in each of the governments should meet for that purpose.[6] The United States delegation had labored for acceptance of such a scheme at the 1936 meeting, but the Argentine delegation had successfully blocked it. The Argentine statesman, Carlos Saavedra Lamas, had derisively referred to such proposed machinery as "an ambulatory Pan American Union."[7]

It was at Lima, in 1938, that the regular Eighth International Conference of American states adopted the means of implementing the consultation agreements for which the United States had argued in vain at Buenos Aires.[8] By 1938 the Hitlerite doctrines of geopolitics and of "perpetual" German citizenship had startled Latin American nations, where thousands of persons of German birth or descended of German blood were to be found. The implications of the Sudeten Crisis were not lost upon these states.

The Republic of Panama had experienced plenty of trouble with Teutonic elements resident on the Isthmus during World War I,[9] and once more had to give attention to the fact that a considerable German ethnic and economic influence existed in the country.

Following World War I the number of Germans in Panama had been considerably increased by immigration from Germany, which got under way soon after the Treaty of Versailles.[10] These people, with typical German industry, soon acquired responsible and influential standing upon the Isthmus. In the fall of 1922 one ex-German, Richard Newman, had been appointed to a high office in the government, and one very well placed for propaganda purposes—Vice-Inspector General of Public Education.[11] In 1924 the government of Panama gave hundreds of acres of fine farm land near Gatun as a free gift to two hundred and fifty families from Germany who came to settle there at its invitation.[12] Thus were the seeds sown for a repetition of 1917 problems as the Americas moved down the pathway toward a second war against Germany.

Furthermore, the situation this time was rendered much more serious than during the first war because Italian and Spanish influences in Latin America were being marshaled to collaborate with the Germans in a great, solid front of fascist activity. Italian undertakings upon the isthmus dated back a number of years,[13] and were linked with a fairly considerable Italian business activity spearheaded by Italian-operated tourist bureaus.[14] The Civil War in Spain had given rise to a *Falangista* party in Panama, and sometimes it was called the *Nacionalista Germano Italiano* party.[15] It operated openly and boldly, and one of its most disquieting techniques was infiltration of schools and establishment of new schools devoted to disseminating its doctrines. In the very year of the Lima Conference Don M. de J. Quijano, a leading Panamanian writer, began to use his pen vigorously to try to arouse his countrymen to *El Peligro de las Escuelas Fascistas* and to advocate the formation of a *Liga Antifascista* in the Republic.[16] His action was by no means a new thing. Liberal-minded Panamanians had already welcomed and furnished asylum to many of the exiles from Franco Spain, and the University of Panama, a center of the Pan American cultural movement, which, together with the University of San

Marcos in Peru, made up the *Instituto Americano Universitario de Investigación,* had placed a number of refugee German scholars upon its faculties.[17]

At Lima Narciso Garay served as Vice-President of the Conference and as Vice-Chairman of the First Committee (Organization of Peace). Panama's other delegates were Jeptha B. Duncan, José B. Lefevre, Manuel M. Valdés, and Ramón L. Vallarino.[18] These men gave strong support to Cordell Hull and the United States delegation in the effort to frame an Inter-American machinery that could effectively oppose either a military or an ideological invasion of the hemisphere.[19]

Some of the delegates from South America, notably from Argentina, Uruguay, Paraguay, and Bolivia, came to Lima entirely unconvinced of any immediate Nazi or Fascist menace. The truth of the matter, of course, is that their attitude was a frightening example of how far sympathy with European totalitarianism had penetrated through the ranks of high government officials in those countries.[20] Their technique at Lima was to work to tone down as much as possible any measures for collective security which the other aroused republics attempted to take. Sumner Welles tells us that the Argentine delegation almost succeeded in disrupting the conference.[21]

After a great deal of behind-the-scenes pressure and persuasion all twenty-one republics were finally brought to agreement in the famous Declaration of Lima on December 24, 1938, whereby the "continental solidarity" of the Western Hemisphere was reaffirmed, and it was proclaimed that a threat to the peace, security, or territorial integrity of any American nation would become a matter of common concern. As noted above the Buenos Aires principle of consultation was now implemented by an agreement that at the invitation of any one of the twenty-one republics the foreign ministers of all should assemble to deliberate what steps should be taken to collectively meet any impending threat.[22]

Panama was naturally interested in the proposal of Dr. Harmodio Arias to create an American Court of International Justice which had been referred to the Commission of Jurists for study at Buenos Aires in 1936.[23] However, the grave immediate issue of foreign aggression overshadowed everything else at Lima and after some debate the Eighth Conference again referred the whole subject of such a court back to the Commission for further study.[24]

With the invasion of Poland the Second World War became a formal reality, and the capital city of Panama found itself the center of the Western Hemisphere, for the first consultative meeting of foreign ministers under the Lima plan was held in Panama City in September 1939. Mexico, on September 5, 1939, suggested to the Government of Panama that the Isthmian Republic take the initiative in inviting the foreign ministers "to bring into operation mutual consultations" and to "put into practice mechanisms" established by various Pan American conferences, and particularly that of 1938 at Lima.

Narciso Garay, Minister of Foreign Affairs, acting in the name of President Juan Demostenes Arosemena, sent out the call for the meeting to be held at Panama City beginning on September 23, 1939. Argentina, Brazil, Chile, Colombia, Cuba, and Peru joined with Mexico and Panama to sponsor the conference. Although the United States does not appear among the official sponsors, it would seem that this was a bit of calculated modesty and that the North American republic had actually played a major role in inspiring the call. Sumner Welles, then U.S. Undersecretary of State, says that Panama was "selected"

THE HEMISPHERE FACES THE AXIS THREAT 93

as the place for this first consultative meeting because of its convenient central location—"an important factor at a time when every day counted." The official call proposed that the state department heads of the twenty-one republics discuss all possible ramifications of the European war which could affect this Hemisphere—its security, economy, and political and social stability.[25]

The Republic of Panama had had personal experience with the very considerable threat to American security posed by the Axis powers. For some time there had been concern over Japanese aims in Central America. The Japanese government had addressed several arrogant and insulting official communications with regard to treatment of Japanese nationals on the Isthmus,[26] and now the German minister began giving out officially offensive publicity releases as soon as President Arosemena's invitations made it evident that Panama was formally initiating the consultation of foreign ministers.[27]

In taking these measures the Axis government displayed a singular inability to appreciate the psychology of Latin American peoples. It is probable that no conduct could have more succeeded in arousing the always intensely patriotic Panamanians to vociferous support of their government. As delegates from the various nations arrived in Panama City they were given flattering ovations everywhere by large and enthusiastic crowds.[28]

President Juan D. Arosemena opened the sessions on the evening of September 23rd at the National Institute.[29] At the close of these ceremonies the delegates went in a body to lay a wreath at the monument of Bolívar, which had been unveiled thirteen years before at the Bolivarian Commemoration Pan American Congress. Narciso Garay, following a custom in Inter-American meetings whereby the host state provides the presiding officer, served as

President of the consultative meetings. Jeptha B. Duncan, of Panama, served as Secretary General. These September days in 1939 were probably the proudest in the history of Panama as an independent state. The Panamanian people were very conscious of the fact that the eyes of the world were upon the deliberations being conducted in their capital city.[30]

The Panama Conference of Foreign Ministers drew a maritime security zone around the twenty-one neutral republics of the hemisphere extending from the waters off Puget Sound to the Galapagos and Cape Horn, and thence around Brazil to Porto Rico and Nova Scotia. Within this zone, which stretched far out into the oceans beyond recognized territorial waters, the respective nations proposed to establish "neutrality patrols," and Panama undertook to notify all belligerents, on behalf of the Inter-American System of states, that maritime hostilities would not be tolerated in this ocean area.[31]

A very practical additional step taken at Panama was the creation of the Inter-American Consultative Economic and Financial Committee, later referred to usually as the "Financial and Economic Advisory Committee."[32] This group wasted no time after the adjournment of the Panama Conference in holding its session, November 15, 1939, in Washington, D. C. Here it recommended the creation of the Inter-American Bank in order that American money and finances might be kept stable and investments facilitated, and the disturbances in trade and finance caused by the war be counteracted as much as possible. The Republic of Panama as a "Group B" member (with a foreign commerce over twenty-five and less than fifty millions of dollars annually) was called upon to subscribe ten shares to the new Bank.[33] The Financial and Economic Committee continued to be a very active body and did important work in the Isthmus of Panama, for it was given cognizance over Axis ships immobilized in American ports and conducted many studies of economic and financial matters.

The Panama Conference also set up the Inter-American Neutrality Committee which was later called the Inter-American Juridical Committee. This group made its principal contribution later, after the actual involvement òf the Americas in hostilities, by making studies of matters which would probably concern this hemisphere in the post-war deliberations connected with the drafting of the peace conventions.[34]

When the fall of France and the Low Countries threatened to jeopardize the security of the Americas by bringing Axis domination over the Western Hemisphere colonial possessions of France and the Netherlands a second meeting of the Foreign Ministers was held at Havana, Cuba, from July 21 to 30, 1940. This session was called in accordance with Resolution XIII of the Panama meeting of the previous year.[35]

The distinguished Narciso Garay again represented his country at a Conference of Foreign Ministers. Ernesto B. Fábrega, Antonio Draizoz, and Raúl Arango N. accompanied him. Señor Garay served as Chairman of the Committee on Credentials, and was also a member of the Committee on Preservation of Peace in the Western Hemisphere.[36] That committee was the most important one of the conference, and it considered a Panamanian project for perfecting the Inter-American mechanism of consultation. The proposal dealt with initiating of such conferences, but there was no substantial agreement for changing the process as set up at Lima and no action was taken.[37]

The Havana Conference adopted an "Act Concerning the Provisional Administration of European Colonies and

Possessions in the Americas," and the "Convention on the Provisional Administration of European Colonies in the Americas." The Convention declared that the American republics would not recognize transfers of colonies in America from one European power to another, and that in the eventuality such a transfer were attempted they would themselves assume administration of such possessions.[38] An Emergency Committee on the Administration of European Colonies and Possessions was created by the Act of Havana, but the most significant part of that document was the carte blanche given to any individual republic to act independently if it considered the emergency too urgent to wait upon the Emergency Committee, so long as it should then place the matter in the hands of the Committee for Legalization.[39] These conventions never had to be employed, but it seems more than likely that they influenced Hitler to hold demands he might otherwise have made upon the French Vichy Government.

Jorge E. Boyd was sent to represent Panama at the first Inter-American Maritime Conference, held in Washington, D. C. from November 25 to December 2 in 1941. The war had of course occasioned a very serious reduction in the tourist trade and Panama had been particularly hard hit by this. Perhaps no other country in the world is more dependent upon the largesse of tourists as a means of redressing its unfavorable balance of trade and making up the difference between exports and imports.[40] It was hoped that some means of stimulating Inter-American travel might come out of this conference—that Americans shut off from accustomed jaunts to Europe might be lured to Latin America instead. In furtherance of this scheme Panama was anxious to get the conference to press the United States to reduce Panama Canal toll transit charges. The North Americans were not willing, however, and so

THE HEMISPHERE FACES THE AXIS THREAT 97

nothing came of this.[41] In the light of the monumental events of the next twelve months, the tourist trade was doomed anyway, and Panama was to experience a bonanza undreamed of at the hands of free spending forces of the United States on the Isthmus, soon to be augmented by many times their normal peacetime complement.

The Japanese attack upon Pearl Harbor, involving an aggression against an American state by an Asiatic power, operated to automatically test the machinery for collective American security which had been forged in the successive conferences dealt with in this chapter. Many of the republics of Latin America, including Panama, followed the United States into a state of declared belligerency almost at once, and throughout the hemisphere the general feeling was that an immediate consultation of foreign ministers was imperative in view of the swift change of so much of America from neutrality to war. At the end of December 1941 the governments of the United States and Chile requested such a meeting and so the Third Conference of Foreign Ministers was called to meet at Rio de Janeiro on January 15, 1942.[42]

The most significant thing to be said about the part played by Panama at the Rio Conference of 1942 is that it was one of the group of states, led by Mexico, Colombia, and Venezuela, which favored, and zealously pushed for, a clean-cut break by the American states with all three Axis powers—Germany, Italy, and Japan.[43] Panama was one of the group that would have been willing to refuse to compromise on the issue, even at the cost of having the Inter-American System fail to present a united front. Octavio Fábrega,[44] Panama's representative and Foreign Minister, was entirely willing to follow the leadership of Mexico's brilliant Foreign Minister, Ezéquiel Padilla,[45] who was the eloquent spokesman of this group. This was the popular course at home too, for Padilla was favorably known and immensely popular in Panama City, as the press accounts in that capital of the Rio proceedings amply demonstrated.[46] Dr. Fábrega himself had spent many years in the United States and like his chief, President de la Guardia, had a reputation in Panama of being very favorably disposed toward the *Yanqui* Republic and anxious to fully collaborate with the Allies in the current war.

Prior to the opening of the conference the Argentine Foreign Minister, Ruiz Guiñazu, had conferred in Buenos Aires with the foreign ministers of Bolivia, Paraguay, Uruguay, and Chile, hoping to organize a bloc to oppose the objectives of the majority of states who wished to make a complete diplomatic, economic, and financial rupture with all three Axis powers. There is no doubt that the Argentine government of the time was completely dominated by the same pro-Fascist elements which we noted as far back as the Lima Conference.[47] Indeed, Acting President Castillo, during the course of the Rio conference, sternly overruled Ruiz Guiñazu, after the Foreign Minister had capitulated to the overwhelming sentiments voiced by the other states to proceed with the proposal of Mexico, Colombia, and Venezuela for a complete break in relations with the Tripartite Powers.[48] In spite of his preliminary cajoleries Ruiz Guiñazu had been unable to persuade Bolivia, Paraguay, or Uruguay to make a common front with Argentina, and only Chile had shown any interest in such a course of action.

Although, as we have stated, there was a strong demand that the nineteen republics favoring the original resolution go ahead and adopt it, leaving Argentina and Chile to their own devices, Sumner Welles, the U.S. delegate, was of the view that a compromise was worth accepting to save the unity upon which he felt certain the future of the Inter-American System would depend. The course advocated by the eloquent and fiery Padilla would in effect have read two republics out of the Pan American family of nations.[49] Consequently Welles was able to persuade the conference to pass a substitute resolution to which Argentina and Chile were willing to adhere, since it merely "recommended" that all of the twenty-one republics sever relations.[50] By the close of the conference, in addition to the thirteen republics who had already declared war on the Axis or broken relations, Brazil, Bolivia, Peru, Uruguay, Paraguay, and Ecuador severed all ties with Germany, Italy, and Japan.[51] Only Argentina and Chile held on to their relations with the Fascist powers.[52]

When the Rio Conference adjourned on January 29, 1942, the intensity of World War II was rapidly being felt among all the states of the hemisphere. The global status of the conflict and the far-flung nature of the Allied combination opposing the Axis, of which Panama was a part, spelled a period of comparative inactivity for a regional organization such as the Inter-American System. During the war years Pan American activity as such held only minor news significance. That of course did not mean that it did not go on. Although no more top-level meetings were to be held until the Chapultepec Conference of 1945, many of the specialized agencies continued their normal functions and the twenty-one republics generally, Panama certainly and wholeheartedly, were determined to keep their hemispheric organization alive. We have already noted the wartime work of the Economic and Financial Advisory Committee and of the Juridical Committee. The Inter-American Committee for Political Defense sponsored consultative visits between the twenty-one republics, and by nature of its strategic location Panama was usually visited in the coming and going of these missions and also by many of the Latin American heads of state who paid good will visits to Washington, D. C., during the war.[53]

In September 1943, Panama was host to the Inter-American Educational Conference,[54] whose sessions centered around the *Universidad Interaméricana*,[55] which was set up in that year by the Panamanian government to operate on the graduate level in international law, and social, economic, and cultural disciplines, with the expressed hope that its scope would be Inter-American and that all of the other twenty republics would contribute to its support.[56] As part of its work in 1943, in conjunction with the U.S. Office of Education, two Panamanian teachers traveled and studied in the United States on funds provided by the Coördinator of Inter-American Affairs.[57] During the war years covered in this chapter Panama also attended conferences of a number of other Inter-American agencies, including the Commission of Women, the Institute of Geography and History, the C.T.A.L. (Latin American Worker's Confederation), the Medical Association, the Commission on Continental Defense composed of military representatives of all the republics, the Congress on Criminology, the Congress on Indian Life, the Inter-American Travel Conference, the Pan American Coffee Congress, the Technical Economic Conference, the Inter-American Bar Association, the Sanitary Congress, the Transportation Congress, the Statistical Congress, and a number of others. Many of them were meeting for the first time, including the Bar Association (at Rio in 1943), the Coffee Congress (at New York in 1940), the Travel Conference (at San Francisco in 1939), the Congress on Criminology (at Santiago in 1944), and the Conference of Commissions on Development (at New York in 1944).[58]

But of much more importance during these years were other conferences which were not "Inter-American," but

THE HEMISPHERE FACES THE AXIS THREAT 101

in which Panama and other Latin American nations were represented and took a prominent part. They were activities of the tremendous project in international coöperation to which in 1942 was applied the name "United Nations," and thus belong in the discussions of the succeeding chapters.

Footnotes

CHAPTER SEVEN

The Hemisphere Faces the Axis Threat

1. Sumner Welles, *The Time for Decision, op. cit.*, p. 205. See also George A. Finch, ed., *Supplement to the International Conferences of American States, op. cit.*, p. 138.
2. Luis Quintanilla, *A Latin American Speaks* (New York, 1943), p. 161.
3. U.S. State Department, *Report of the Delegation of the United States of America to the Inter-American Conference for the Maintenance of Peace at Buenos Aires, Argentina*, December 1-23, 1936 (Washington, 1937), p. 45.
4. Juan Antonio Susto, *Compilación, Indices y Notas: Leyes expedidas por la Asamblea Nacional de Panamá, 1938* (Panamá, 1939), pp. 51-113.
5. *Ibid.*, p. 81.
6. Charles G. Fenwick, "The Inter-American Conference for the Maintenance of Peace," *American Journal of International Law*, Vol. 31, April, 1937, p. 203.
7. Welles, *supra*, p. 209.
8. U.S. State Department, *Report of the Delegation of the United States of America to the Eighth International Conference of American States, Lima, Peru, December 9-27, 1938* (Washington, 1941), pp. 189-90.
9. See Chapter Four, *supra*, pp. 45, 46, 48.
10. U.S. State Department, Dispatch 2939, from Price, at Panama, April 11, 1921.
11. U.S. State Department, Dispatch, from South, at Panama, rec'd. by telegram at 5 p.m., November 5, 1922.

12. U.S. State Department, Dispatch 403, from South, at Panama, March 20, 1924.
13. U.S. State Department, Dispatch 806, from Bucknell, at Panama, November 6, 1931, to Stimson, reporting pro-Fascist celebrations of Italians on the isthmus.
14. M. de J. Quijano, "Una Campaña Antifascista," in Vol. I of his work, *En la Ruta Liberal y Democrática* (Panamá, 1943), pp. 2, 97.
15. *Ibid.*, pp. 42, 46.
16. *Ibid.*, pp. 45, 46, 94.
17. Samuel Guy Inman, *Building an Inter-American Neighborhood* (New York, 1937), p. 46.
18. Finch, ed., *Supplement to Conferences, supra*, p. 227.
19. Samuel G. Inman, *The Lima Conference and the Totalitarian Issue*, Annals of the American Academy of Political Sciences, Vol. 204, July 1939, pp. 119-25.
20. See article, "Nazidom at Lima," *New Republic Magazine*, for December 7, 1938, pp. 97, 127-28.
21. Sumner Welles, *The Time for Decision, op. cit.*, p. 208.
22. *U.S. Department of State Bulletin*, No. 1, 1939, pp. 20, 287, 326, 660. See also *Bulletin of the Pan American Union*, LXXIII (Washington, 1939), pp. 68, 129.
23. See Chapter Six, p. 80, *supra*.
24. Finch, *Supplement to Conferences, supra*, p. 144n.
25. *Ibid.*, p. 315n.
26. Panama has long adhered to Oriental exclusion and restrictive policies similar to those of the U.S.A. This has often caused trouble and bitterness upon the Isthmus and in international relations. See Paul Blanshard, *Democracy and Empire in the Caribbean* (New York, 1947), pp. 369-70; Luis Marden, "Panama, Bridge of the World," *op. cit.*, p. 600; and Farnham Bishop, *Panama, Past and Present* (New York, 1916), p. 204. On the Japanese question see Carleton Beals, *The Coming Struggle for Latin America* (Philadelphia, 1938), pp. 13-18.
27. Welles, *supra*, p. 210.
28. The *Panama Star and Herald*, and the *Panama American*, for September 15-22, 1939.
29. *Talleres Gráficos* reprinted the President's welcoming address for circulation in an eight-page pamphlet, "Discurso pronunciado por el presidente de la República de Panamá, doctor Juan Demostenes Arosemena, en la sesión inaugural de la reunión consultiva de los ministros de las Repúblicas Americas" (Panamá, 1939).

30. *Panama Star and Herald,* and *Gaceta Oficial,* for September 22–October 5, 1939.

31. Pan American Union, *Acta final de la Reunión de Consulta entre los Ministros de Relaciones Exteriores de las Repúblicas Américanas en Panama* (Panamá, 1939). See also *Bulletin* (Washington, D. C.), of May 1940, pp. 403, 404-5, 406-7.

32. Pan American Union, Comité Consultivo Económico Financiero Interaméricano, *Manual de su organización y actividades 1939-1943* (Washington, 1943). Also John P. Humphrey, *The Inter-American System, op. cit.,* p. 214.

33. Reynolds, *Progress of Pan Americanism, op. cit.,* p. 387.

34. Pan American Union, Inter-American Juridical Committee, *Preliminary Recommendation on Post War Programs* (Washington, 1942). See also Welles, *supra,* p. 213. Also, U.S. State Department, *Report of the Delegate of the United States of America to the Meeting of the Foreign Ministers of the American Republics at Panama, September 23–October 3, 1939* (Washington, 1940), p. 57.

35. Finch, *Supplement to Conferences, op. cit.,* p. 343.

36. República de Panamá, Secretaría de Relaciones Exteriores, *Memoria 1938-1940* (Panamá, 1942), p. LI.

37. T. H. Reynolds, *Progress of Pan Americanism, supra,* p. 18.

38. Pan American Union, *Report on the Second Meeting of the Foreign Ministers* (Washington, 1940), p. 6.

39. U.S. State Department, *Report of the Delegate of the United States to the Second Meeting of the Ministers of Foreign Affairs of the American Republics, Havana, Cuba, July 21-30, 1940* (Washington, 1941), pp. 75-77.

40. For statistics on Panamanian trade during World War II, see Arthur P. Whitaker, ed., *Inter-American Affairs 1945, Annual Survey No. 5, op. cit.,* p. 258, showing exports of $4,507,000 and imports of $45,648,000 for 1944. For compilation of wartime economic statistics in some detail see the Dun and Bradstreet publication, Alexander O. Stanley, ed., *A Geo-Economic Study of Latin America, op. cit.*

41. T. H. Reynolds, *supra.* p. 98.

42. *U.S. State Department Bulletin,* No. V, 1942, pp. 129-131.

43. Welles, *The Time for Decision, op. cit.,* p. 417. Sumner Welles was the U.S. representative at Rio and his account is thus probably the most authoritative now available. It is a fairly full résumé of the Conference (pp. 219-35 and 415-17).

44. Señor Fábrega was the law partner of the distinguished statesman, Harmodio Arias. He was an exponent of the Calvo Doctrine and an outstanding leader of the Liberal element in Pan-

ama. He had particularly close ties with Mexico and had been decorated by that country. See Ronald Hilton, ed., *Who's Who in Latin America*, Part II, "Central America and Panama" (Stanford University, Palo Alto, 1945), p. 89.

45. See Ezéquiel Padilla, *Free Men of America* (Chicago, 1943), for his philosophy toward the international menace of fascism.

46. Panama *Star and Herald*, and the *American*, January 15-30, 1942.

47. See W. L. Shirer, "Hitler's Latin American Front," *The Nation*, CLIV, p. 463, April 18, 1942; Laurence and Silvia Martin, "Nazi Intrigues in South America," American Mercury, LIII, pp. 66-73, July, 1941.

48. Welles, *The Time for Decision, op. cit.*, p. 232.

49. *Ibid.*, p. 233.

50. Pan American Union, *Report on the Third Meeting of the Ministers of Foreign Affairs of the American Republics, Rio de Janeiro, January 15-28, 1942* (Washington, 1942), p. 32.

51. *New York Times*, January 25-30, 1942.

52. See John P. Humphrey, "Argentina's Diplomatic Victory," *Canadian Forum*, XXI, pp. 362-64, March, 1942. The "solid American front" did become a reality, belatedly, when Chile severed diplomatic relations in January, 1943, and Argentina, finally, in January, 1944.

53. Typical was the visit of President Prado, of Peru, in 1942, which is commemorated, with many pictorial illustrations in the official publication, *Ideario y acción panaméricanistas del Presidente Prado. Estados Unidos, Cuba, Panamá, Venezuela, Colombia* (Lima, 1944).

54. El Diario Nacional, *Conferencia de Ministros y Directores de Educación de las Repúblicas Americanas. Primera* (Panamá, 1943).

55. Ernesto J. Castillero R., ed., *La Universidad Interaméricana. Historia de sus antecedentes y fundación* (Panamá, 1943).

56. Victor F. Goytía, *El Liberalismo y la Constitución* (Panamá), pp. 75-76. See also pamphlet of Ministerio de Educación, *Programa de Estudios superiores de los Institutos* (Panamá, 1944), 48 pp.

57. Whitaker, ed., *Inter-American Affairs, 1943, supra*, p. 173.

58. República de Panamá, Ministerio de Relaciones Exteriores, *Memoria 1943-1944* (Panamá, 1945), pp. lviii, lxi. Also Ruth T. Masters, ed., Carnegie Endowment for International Peace, *Handbook of International Organizations in the Americas* (New York, 1945); and the Pan American Union's *Inter-American Conferences, 1826-1948* (Washington, 1949).

CHAPTER EIGHT

The Isthmian Republic in World War II

As THE GENERAL European War involved much of the world in the gloomy autumn of 1939, the Republic of Panama issued a formal proclamation of neutrality on September 11th.[1] A proclamation by the United States on September 5th had already established the neutral status of the Canal Zone.[2] The interpretation of the Hull-Alfaro Treaty now became a matter of pressing necessity. Articles I, II, and X of this agreement pledged Panama and the United States to coöperate and to take necessary military measures *in the territory of Panama* in the event of any emergency endangering the Republic or the neutrality or security of the Canal Zone.

At the time of senatorial consent to ratification of the treaty U.S. Senator Key Pitman of Nevada, Chairman of the Foreign Relations Committee of the Senate, had stated that the United States would *unilaterally* determine when an emergency would require consultation or action.[3] It had been this semipledge from a high authority, in fact, which had finally influenced many wavering senators to vote for ratification. The uneasy feeling that the renunciation of rights held under the old Hay-Bunau-Varilla Treaty might prejudice the ability of the United States to defend the Canal in some future emergency had for a time threatened to defeat the treaty. The Roosevelt Administration had sought by public assurances from Secretary Hull and others to assuage this fear on the domestic political scene, but had also had to employ the most carefully chosen words in order not to arouse anti-*Yanqui* doubts and resentments in Panama.[4] No one in the executive branch therefore either affirmed or denied the pronouncement of Senator Pitman. However, the course of conduct actually pursued by the Roosevelt Administration from 1939 to 1942 was always one of mutual consultation with Panama and action based always upon agreement reached with the Isthmian government.

During the period of uneasy neutrality after September, 1939, the two republics generally followed the precedents of the similar period between 1914 and 1917 with respect to extending hospitality to belligerent war vessels in the waters of both Panama and the Canal Zone. The Roosevelt Administration very early signed an executive agreement with Panama which very largely reaffirmed the Lansing-Morales Protocol of 1914.[5]

From September, 1939, to December 7, 1941, the governments of Panama and the United States collaborated very closely upon the Isthmus. In general Panama followed the lead of the United States in straining traditional concepts of "neutrality." The Isthmian government even permitted British naval authorities to hospitalize a German prisoner at Santo Tomás Hospital in the City of Panama and then return him under guard on board a British war vessel at Balboa[6]—a great violence to the long-held rule of international law that entry of a belligerent national into a neutral state entitled him to claim the benefits of internment. Nor did Panama raise any objection when the Lend-Lease program of the United States resulted in military aid to Allied forces in Canal Zone ports—a clear violation of the guarantee given to Panama by the Treaty of 1903 that the Canal would be kept neutral in perpetuity.⁷

The order of President Roosevelt on March 30, 1941, for the seizure of the Axis vessels in American waters caught the Italian luxury liner *Conte Biancamano* in Cristobal. It was boarded and seized by U.S. marshals acting under the executive order and also by authority of libel action filed by the Panama Canal authorities in the U.S. District Court at Balboa.⁸ This action reiterated the principle determined during World War I that the commitments of 1903 by the United States to Panama to keep the Canal perpetually neutral could not be relied upon by any *third* power to be interpreted in any fashion which the United States would deem inimical to her own interests.

The acquiescence of the Panamanian government in openly "un-neutral" acts of the United States was virtually dictated by the prevailing public opinion within the Republic. Ricardo J. Alfaro was an eloquent spokesman for the Panamanian distrust of the Axis—a distrust which fed upon the fact that, as he said in June, 1941: "One third of the states of the World—21 peace-loving, proud sovereign nations have had their soil invaded and their independence destroyed."⁹

The same statesman was bitterly cynical of Japanese claims during that fatal summer of 1941 that they were striving to reach a "peaceful" solution of conflicting claims and interests in Greater East Asia and the Pacific. "Imagine . . . a sweet loving dove (referring to Japan) by whose tender caresses of steel and fire over 2,000,000 Chinese have perished!"¹⁰

One of the immediate results of Panama's predominately pro-Allied sentiment was seen in the use of her flag to circumvent the restrictions of the United States Neutrality Law, which in 1939 excluded United States ships from all war zones. Panama had no such law. Many U.S. shipowners, lured by the immense profits to be gained by carrying war materials, hastened to change the registry of their vessels to the Panamanian flag so that they might be sailed into belligerent waters. Panama's merchant marine, only 300,000 tons in 1939, soon was climbing to over 2,000,000 tons.[11] Since this carrying trade was exclusively in the interest of the Allies it may truthfully be said that the Panamanian colors were the first of any Pan American nation to fly over major operations designed to bring about the defeat of the Axis. As the United States drifted toward more and more open support of the Allies the Washington government encouraged this use of Panamanian shipping. Indeed, even before the Act of November 17, 1941, allowed the arming of United States Merchantmen, the U.S. Navy had quietly placed defensive installations on board North American-owned ships of Panamanian registry.[12]

By a law of January 12, 1925, it was provided that all "national vessels engaged in international traffic" were required to employ Panamanian citizens in a proportion at least to 10 per cent of their crews. There thus can be no doubt but that Panamanian lives as well as ships were committed to the deadly task of carrying munitions, petroleum products, tanks, and other implements of war to Europe.

Although this direct involvement of the Panamanian flag and of Isthmian nationals in the toils of the World War had the support of the press, of many distinguished leaders of public opinion, and probably of a majority of Panamanian citizens, it was far from pleasing to certain very voluble elements within the Republic. Attention has already been devoted to the existence of German ethnic groups in the Panamanian population,[13] and to the activities of Fascist groups in Panama which had caused concern as far back as the Lima Conference of 1938. German planters and storekeepers were heavily spotted along the coasts of the Gulf of Darien, as well as in Panama City and Colón, and German agents disguised as traders and mahogany cutters were known by U.S. Naval Intelligence to have penetrated many sections of the interiors.[14] It was also known that Italian "tourist" activities covered many sinister operations and that often personnel of luxury liners such as the *Conte Biancamano* were actually Italian naval officers who charted coastal waters, took photographs, etc.

After the formal entry of Catholic and Latin Italy into the conflict, totalitarian activities in Panama became more and more brazen. The *Hispanidad* movement, stimulated by the diplomatic and consular officers of Franco Spain, stepped up operations until local posts of *Falangistas* were serving in nearly every town to disseminate Axis propaganda, stir up anti-*Yanqui* hatreds, and report military information through their network to the Tri-Partite powers.[15]

Arnulfo Arias, brother of Ex-President Harmodio Arias, and his *Nacionalistas*, whether designedly or not, found themselves vociferously supported by the *Hispanidad* elements, although it must be allowed that there were many *Nacionalistas* who were sincere patriotic citizens, not concerned with the Axis, or the Allies, but only with Panama's sovereign independence, and who sought to turn the world situation to Panama's economic advantage by insisting upon the prerogatives of juridical international equality and by driving hard bargains with the Allies and particularly the United States. It may very well be that Arias himself was moved by such sentiments, but he found himself judged by the company he was keeping, in October 1940, when President Arosemena died suddenly and he accepted

Hispanidad support in his successful campaign for the vacant presidency.

President Arias soon became *persona non grata* to North American and anti-Axis quarters by making numerous speeches which were interpreted an "anti-*Yanqui.*" A re-reading of them at the time of this writing, ten years later, shows them not to be so much anti-anything or anybody as intensely, vociferously nationalistic or pro-Panamanian. It seems significant to this writer that he did, despite cries about his "hostility" toward the United States, grant the Washington government permission to take over sites for air bases and other defense purposes.[16] His opposition to the proposal to arm U.S.-owned ships flying the flag of Panama, and his threat to stop such vessels from sailing to war zones, when considered from the *Panamanian,* rather than from the anti-Axis point of view, could have been legitimate efforts by the head of a sovereign and independent state to preserve the declared neutrality of the state. The granting of the base sites to the United States was a faithful performance of all that Panama was required by treaty commitments to do. At no time had she agreed to permit her national flag to mask operations of great powers on the high seas or to be used as a pawn in Allied prosecution of the war. Of course it cannot be denied that this show of Panamanian independence did give aid and comfort to the Nazis and their allies by the mere fact that it discomfited their enemies. Señor Arias has always insisted, however, that this was an incidental *consequence,* and not at all the *purpose,* of his acts.

A bloodless revolution in October 1941, while Arias was absent in Cuba, overthrew his regime and brought in as new President of the Republic Ricardo de la Guardia, a former Minister of Justice and ostentatiously friendly toward both the United States and the Allies. He was supported by the coalition of political parties which embraced these views and were anti-fascist—the Socialists, the National Revolutionary, the Liberal, the National Liberal, the Democratic, the United Liberal, the Conservative, and the Reform Liberal parties.[17] Although it was denied by Washington, the friends of Arias bitterly charged the United States with having directly instigated this revolt. This writer was in Panama just after the affair and was solemnly assured by the daughter of a former Minister of Government that the editor of one of the capital newspapers organized the uprising on telephoned instructions from the U.S. Department of State! Needless to say there is no way for me to confirm or disprove this charge. I repeat it merely to show the state of at least one section of opinion in Panama after the event. Secretary Hull was sufficiently concerned by the welter of charges and countercharges to declare that the United States did not know of the plot and was not involved in it either directly or indirectly.[18] Since Mr. Hull obviously could not know for certain what some, or one, of his associates may have been doing *subrepticiamente,* it is understandable that many Panamanians remained unconvinced of *Yanqui* innocence.

The de la Guardia regime was presented almost immediately with an opportunity to demonstrate its friendship toward the United States, for within a few weeks the Pearl Harbor attack had propelled the United States into open belligerency and the Declaration of Lima and the assurances of the Hull-Alfaro negotiations alike were put to the acid test. Panama at once declared war upon the three principal Axis powers then at war with the United States. As in World War I, the Isthmian Republic had become a partner in a gigantic coöperative enterprise to win a global conflict.

In moves remindful of 1917 the Republic collaborated

with North American authorities from the Canal Zone in rounding up nationals and suspected agents of enemy powers. The most stringent regulations were adopted with respect to control of foreigners residing upon the isthmus, immigration rules provided for close scrutiny of all persons coming from Axis or Axis-occupied lands and claiming to be political refugees, and Panama collaborated very closely with Canal Zone authorities in restricting travel and communications in areas which had been declared to be restricted, military, or security zones.[19] For a time Axis nationals were held in a stockade at Fort Amador in Balboa, and then, following the precedents of World War I, were all transported to the United States for internment. After V-J Day those who had been seized upon Panamanian soil were returned there.

Not only were *Yanqui* forces in the Canal Zone greatly augmented, but additional troops garrisoned strategic points throughout the Republic by agreement with de la Guardia's administration. U.S. military officers were established in liaison billets in the offices of the Panamanian government where such advisory aid would further wartime administration.[20] U.S. Naval patrols were welcomed at many points, such as the Perlas Islands in Panama Bay, and off Cape Malo. Local Germans were believed to have been organized in remote coastal settlements in Bocas del Toro to send out fresh provisions to U-Boats by means of small craft. Captain Morison tells us that one of the Navy's most exasperating tasks was the constant patrol of every "river mouth, reef-protected anchorage, or mangrove-lined creek where a U-Boat might possibly hide out or procure drummed fuel."[21] Vast efforts were made to reduce the dangers from air raids regarded as certain to come from secret bases in the remote jungles of neighboring states, or from Japanese aircraft carriers or submarines. Morison

ISTHMIAN REPUBLIC IN WORLD WAR II   113

says that until 1944 military and naval leadership considered the Japanese the greatest potential threat to Panama, despite the German U-Boat campaign in the Caribbean.[22] This is indeed revealing, and, in view of Captain Morison's position as official Naval Historian, authoritative. The officials of the Republic coöperated vigorously in an isthmian blackout, regulation of motor vehicle traffic, rationing of certain critical commodities, and mail, telephone, and telegraph censorship.[23] Even the movements of small fishing vessels along a twenty-mile stretch of coast extending away from the Canal entrances on both Atlantic and Pacific sides were completely suspended in order to assure the security of the Canal installations. A strict prohibition was also enforced against the taking of soundings or other geodetic surveys by private vessels in Panamanian territorial waters.[24] In almost every way the all-out character of the Second World War was more keenly felt in Panama than any phase of World War I.

This writer resided on the Isthmus from December 1941 to October 1942, and has many personal recollections of the general intensity of feeling for the Allied cause among the Panamanian people.[25] Pictures of Roosevelt and Churchill adorned every public place as well as innumerable private homes and even *chivas* (Panamanian version of a jitney bus). The black news of the winter of 1941-42—the fall of Singapore, Manila, and Batavia, and Rommel's advance into Egypt—was reflected in the public consciousness in a thousand forms. North American service men stationed in Panama or passing through the Canal en route to Pacific battlefields were treated with a cordiality very striking in contrast with a traditional suspicion and coolness which often greeted military personnel of the United States in pre-war days. In the *cantinas* of remote towns and villages I often saw the convivial spirit of pro-Allied sympathy expressed in flowery toasts to the United Nations and their leaders.

Panamanians worked by the thousands around the clock on numerous war projects—the third locks at Miraflores, the Trans-Isthmian and David highways,[26] and the greatly expanded U.S. military and naval installations at West Balboa, Howard Field, Forts Kobe and Clayton, and Taboga.[27] Without this willing labor pool the Allies might have experienced much more difficulty than they did in recovering from the shocks of the early Japanese victories and Nazi U-Boat successes. This was emphasized in the fuel crisis of 1942. Fuel deliveries to the Pacific depended upon the use of tankers coming from Aruba, Curaçao, and Gulf ports by way of the Panama Canal. Fuel oil was an absolute prerequisite for Pacific operations of the U.S. Navy and the Army Air Force. During the summer of 1942 German U-Boats in the Caribbean took such a toll of the tanker fleet that a pipe line was hastily constructed across the isthmus to eliminate the Canal bottleneck and enable the fast Pacific tankers to make a quick turn-around by loading at Balboa. Thousands of Panamanians were employed in this $20,000,000 project.[28]

President de la Guardia neglected no opportunity to exhort his people to contribute in every possible way to the winning of the war. The radio station HB50G in Panama City, styling itself *La Voca de Democracia,* beamed out all sorts of patriotic broadcasts containing official statements of Panama's vital stake in the United Nations cause. Under the leadership of Dr. Jesús Vásquez Gayoso, Director of the Universidad del Aire of the National Institute, some of the best of these have been collected together and published by the government in a widely disseminated volume entitled *Una Nación en Guerra.*[29] The following subjects of some of the addresses indicate the general tenor of this work, which has generally been considered to have been tremendously influential in molding public opinion within the Republic: "Generalities on Civil Defense," "Fundamentals of Democracy," "Espionage," "Biological Warfare," "Aviation and Air Attacks," "The Woman in War," "Food in War," "The American Objective in this War," "Business Affairs and War," and "The Fifth Column."

The government emphasized over and over that Panama's contribution to victory against the Axis powers would likely lie in auxiliary services—"the prevention of enemy infiltrations, maintenance of eternal alertness, aiding the transport and communications of United States forces, furnishing them hospitality and other assistance, and civic collaboration in measures to defend the Canal."[30]

One phase of the national contribution could not be publicized for security reasons, but it involved the heroic carrying of vital war supplies to Russia. Panamanian vessels were used in the North Russia convoys and Panamanian sons and the national colors of the Republic were in action in one of the hottest theaters of the war.[31] Some were lost to enemy action. Even to this day it is not generally known that the isthmian state had personnel and and vessels in this dangerous mission to Murmansk and Archangel. One of the most fearful ordeals of the war was the famous attack on Convoy "PQ-17," bound from Iceland to Archangel. This flotilla was under attack for days along the Norwegian coast, the high point coming on July 4, 1942. In that battle the Panamanian freighter *S.S. Earlston* was sunk with the loss of most of its crew. Another Panamanian vessel, *S.S. Troubadour*, was saved largely by the resourcefulness of its Master, George J. Salvesen, who camouflaged her among the ice floes by painting her sides white and spreading bed and table linen over superstructures. In that onslaught the Allies lost twenty-two out of thirty-three ships in the convoy.[32]

As has been noted earlier in this work, Panama is fundamentally a food-importing nation. When the German U-Boat blitz in the Caribbean and Gulf of Mexico during the summer of 1942 seriously reduced the staple stocks of the isthmus there was no grumbling or loss of faith on the part of the Panamanian people, but a determined tightening of the belt and a willingness to sacrifice coveted foodstuffs and other strategic materials to the primary need of feeding the vast *Gringo* military establishment upon the isthmus that was very touching.[33] The extent of the hardship is difficult to measure because of the good grace with which it was endured, but many merchants and business firms must have been close to ruin, and even the great daily newspapers were almost forced to close down because of inability to get newsprint from abroad.

Prior to the Battle of the Coral Sea it was considered probable that the southern prong of the great Japanese offensive moving east over the Pacific would be aimed at Panama. Panama's only effective avenue of communication with the United States was by sea. The Caribbean U-Boat offensive seemed timed to coincide with the Japanese Pacific assault. It seemed possible that Panama might be cut off from the rest of North America should the Axis effort come near success. Both the government and the people considered this possibility in their planning, and all organs of official opinion made it clear that the national plan was to emulate the courageous Filipinos in resisting Axis landings if they came.

Accordingly, the following organizations were mobilized and trained in various tasks for the *defensa continental*: the *Batallones de Cadetes*, composed of young men still in the various secondary schools of the country, where military training was made part of the curriculum; the *Cuerpo de Exploradres* (a body of Scout organizations); the *Mujeres Guías* (female Scouts); *Brigadas de la Cruz Roja* (Red Cross); and the *Milicias Nacionales y Cuerpos Auxiliares*. By decree of the de la Guardia Administration (Number 431 of June 6, 1942), these groups were placed under the direction of a unified military command. All of these units took great pride in their work and organization and the *Batallón Primero del Istmo,* a force of five hundred based in Panama City itself, became a crack outfit, often appearing in patriotic reviews and demonstrations. Lieutenant Colonel José A. Remón headed the staff, or *Junta Superior,* which directed these operations. Other members were Francisco Aued, Oscar Ocana, and Lieutenant Colonel William Wedemeyer, liaison officer of the U.S. Army.

The U.S. Army coöperated very closely in training and equipping Panamanian forces. Of particular usefulness and service was the Panama Beach Watch in Chiriqui Province, whose mission was to "observe and investigate suspicious activity on the beaches, the approaches thereto, the offshore waters, the adjacent border, and the air overhead." A U.S. Army force of four officers and twenty-three enlisted men, all fluent in the Spanish language, was detailed to serve with this beach patrol command.[34]

The Battle of Midway ended the threat from the West, but Captain Morison says that until about 1944 the U.S. military and naval authorities estimated that Japanese submarine or carrier raids were a principal menace to the Panama Canal, and that all planning for the strategic defense of the Caribbean area was predicated upon this assumption.[35]

In 1942 the de la Guardia Administration made an

agreement to turn over to the United States further defense base sites outside the Canal Zone "for not more than one year after hostilities shall cease."[36] The principal ones were the B-29 airfield at Rio Hato, with 20,000 acres and a 9,000-foot runway; army radar stations in the Perlas Islands and at other internal locations, and the Navy's P.T. boat base at Taboga Island.[37] In exchange for these bases the North Americans assumed Panama's unpaid debt on the Chorerra Rio Hato highway and the bonds of the Colón and Panama City waterworks and sewage systems.[38] A further act implementing the joint war program of the two republics was the program of the United States Board of Economic Warfare and of the Defense Supplies Corporation, which planted over 6,500 acres of hemp-producing abaca in the Bocas del Toro region, shipped millions of pounds of seeds from there for further cultivation in Costa Rica and Honduras, developed the export of mahogany woods for war purposes, and put thousands of additional acres to rice and corn production to relieve the drain on the isthmian food supply.[39] Still another measure was the granting to the U.S. Rubber Development Corporation of a complete monopoly on Panama's output of crude rubber.[40]

All of the foregoing programs of the two governments had to face the unyielding and violent opposition of Nationalist, *Hispanidad,* and anti-*Gringo* elements, which used every means of sabotage within their power. At times their activity was notorious enough to evoke despairing comments from Allied partisans such as this statement by M. de J. Quijano in his *Una Campaña Antifascista* published in 1943:

¡a pesar de que Panamá hace parte de las Naciones Unidas, el fascismo vive, el nacismo vive, el falangismo vive, en la patria de Tomás Herrera![41]

In spite of their noise, however, the schemes of these fanatics were entirely frustrated. Intelligence officers had done an excellent job. Most plots were known in advance of their intended execution and were easily dealt with by Canal Zone or Panamanian authorities. In this task of counter-espionage, I have been told by fellow naval officers of the Intelligence Service that the patriotic Panamanians came forward in almost every instance to inform on their backsliding countrymen and made the task of keeping effective security measures infinitely easier.

After 1944, when the growing Allied seapower had finally broken the back of Germany's U-Boat fleet in the Atlantic, the Caribbean area became a "quiet zone" in a world at war. The contribution of the Republic of Panama to the United Nations war effort was then complete except for providing logistic services and morale-building shore leave, as the last outpost of "civilization," to military forces transiting the Canal en route to Pacific battle areas. Times had seen a great change from the gloomy days of spring 1942, when it had seemed very possible that the Isthmus would become a primary war zone where the Western Hemisphere would be fighting a last ditch struggle for its very freedom. The American states had contributed enormously to the turn of the tide.[42] In retrospect Panama, one of the world's smallest nations, could look back with understandable pride and satisfaction upon her role in this titanic war. In the words of one of her own governmental spokesmen she could declare:

... Entonces, capacitados en lo moral y en lo material para ser auxiliares efectivos de la defensa del Istmo, del Canal y de las Américas, nuestros aliados nos verán con respeto, nuestros hijos hablarán de nosotros con admiración y la frase "Panamá esta en guerra" habrá cobrado su verdadera connotación histórica.[43]

Footnotes

CHAPTER EIGHT

The Isthmian Republic in World War II

1. The *Panama Star and Herald*, September 11-12, 1939.
2. Norman J. Padelford, *The Panama Canal in Peace and War*, op. cit., pp. 159-67.
3. U.S. *Congressional Record* (76th Congress, First Session, 1939), pp. 9833-37.
4. U.S. *Department of State Bulletin*, Vol. I of 1939, p. 84 et seq.
5. See Chapter Four, pp. 40-41. Also Padelford, p. 158, and Ricardo J. Alfaro, *Los Acuerdos entre Panamá y los Estados Unidos* (Panamá, 1943), 12 pp.
6. This episode occurred while the German merchantman, *Duesseldorf*, with a British prize crew, transited the Canal. The German Consul at Colón protested. See the *New York Times* for December 26-27, 1939, and January 22, 1940.
7. U.S. *Department of State Bulletin*, Vol. IV of 1941, p. 85 et seq.
8. *Ibid*. p. 420. Also the New York Times for March 31, April 15, and August 31, 1941. The *Conte Biancamano* was renamed the USS *Hermitage*, and was used as a troop transport during the war. On November 15, 1948, the ship was officially turned back to the Italian government. More than $3,500,000 was spent to restore her as a luxury liner and she was put in service between New York and Naples in the spring of the Holy Year (1950).
9. Quoting from an address delivered at Oklahoma A. and M. College, Stillwater, Oklahoma, June 19, 1941, and printed in T. H. Reynolds, *The Progress of Pan Americanism*, op. cit., p. 158.
10. *Ibid*.
11. These figures are taken from an article by Sydney Gruson, "Panama Deflects Shipping Boycott," in the *New York Times* for August 31, 1949.
12. Samuel E. Morison, Capt. USNR, *The Battle of the Atlantic* (New York, 1947), p. 297.
13. See Chapter Four, p. 42, and Chapter Seven, pp. 89-91, *supra*.

14. Morison, *supra*, p. 150.
15. M. de J. Quijano, *Una Campañ Antifascista, 1937-1940, op. cit.* See p. 5 ("Arrival of Franco Ambassador"); p. 14 ("Fascist Propaganda in Panama"); p. 45 ("El Peligro de las Escuelas Fascistas"); p. 97 ("Italian Activity on the Isthmus"); pp. 111 and 151-53 ("The Struggle in Panama between *Hispanismo and Panamericanismo*").
16. Austin F. MacDonald, *Latin American Politics and Government, op. cit.*, p. 614.
17. Victor F. Goytía, *El Liberalismo y la Constitución* (Panamá, 1945), p. 195.
18. MacDonald, *supra*, p. 614.
19. Karl Lowenstein, ed., Comité Consultivo de Emergencia para la defensa politica publicación. *Legislación Para la Defensa Politica en las Repúblicas Américanas*, 2 vols. (Montevideo, 1947), Tomo I, pp. 97, 113, 510, 601, 636, 703, and 707. See also Padelford, *The Panama Canal in Peace and War, op. cit.*, p. 175; and the Panama *Star and Herald*, December 8-15, 1941.
20. U.S. State Department, *U.S. Treaties Series, 1933-1945* (F. D. Roosevelt), Exec. Series No. 414, Department of State Publication 2202, Exchange of notes signed at Washington, D. C., April 26 and May 18, 1944, continuing in effect the agreement of July 7, 1942, as extended by agreement of July 6 and August 5, 1943.
21. Morison, *The Battle of the Atlantic, supra*, pp. 150-51.
22. *Ibid.*, p. 149.
23. Lowenstein, ed., *Legislación para la Defensa*, etc., *supra*, Tome II, pp. 195, 203, and 207. Censorship followed the precedents of World War I, and was generally directed by U.S. authorities. This writer, then on active duty in the U.S. Navy, at times was assigned Spanish language censorship duties at activities of the 15th Naval District in Balboa. This subject is thoroughly reported in the War Diary of the 15th Naval District, Office of Naval Records and Library. This is, however, a classified file of manuscript material and may as yet only be examined by qualified persons.
24. Lowenstein, *supra*, Tomo II, pp. 493-501.
25. In this connection attention is invited to a pamphlet published under auspices of the Minister of Propaganda: Octavio Méndez Pereira, ed., *Acción democrática internacional, tres fechas* (Panamá, 1943), 70 pp.
26. U.S. State Department, *U.S. Treaties Series, 1933-1945* (F. D. Roosevelt), Exec. Series No. 448, Trans-Isthmian Highway Agreement between the U.S.A. and Panama. See also Tomlinson, *The Other Americans, op. cit.*, pp. 143-44.

27. U.S. Navy Department, Bureau of Yards and Docks publication, *Building the Navy's Bases in World War II*, contains a very informative account of the defense installations erected in Panama. See Vol. II. (Washington, 1947), Chapter 18, Part II, "The Canal Zone," pp. 15-22.

28. *Ibid.*, p. 19.

29. Jesús Vázquez Gayoso, ed., *Una Nación en Guerra* (Panamá, 1947).

30. *Ibid.* See p. 291, reprint of radio address by Felipé Juan Escobar, Professor of Procedural Law in the University of Panama.

31. Morison, *The Battle of the Atlantic, op. cit.*, pp. 179-92, and 367.

32. Interview between Carlos Berguido, Jr., Panama Consul General at Philadelphia and Captain Salvesen, reported to this writer by Señor Berguido. This incident is also noted in the report of Ensign H. E. Carraway, USNR, Armed Guard Officer, Convoy PQ-17, filed November 5, 1942, Navy Department, Office of Naval Records and Library.

33. As an example of the harsh effects of war upon the Panamanian economy see Scott Seegers, "The World's Best Business Set-Up," *op. cit.*, pp. 14 and 32. On the seriousness of the German U-Boat operations in the Caribbean see H. B. Murkland, "Attack Stirs Costa Rica," *Current History*, September 1942, p. 53. Also the *Official Communiques of the U.S. Navy* (Washington, 1946), Numbers 63, 64, 81, and 129.

34. Victor F. Goytía, *La Función Geografica del Istmo, op. cit.*, Chap. X, "Panamá Cumple su Misión," 160, 161, and 164; and Chap. XI, "La Juventud ante La Guerra," pp. 193, 194, and 196-208.

35. Morison, *supra*, p. 149.

36. U.S. State Department, *U.S. Treaties Series, 1933-1945* (F. D. Roosevelt), Exec. Agreement Series No. 359, Department of State publ. 2106 (Washington, 1944), Lease of defense base sites, signed May 18, 1942.

37. Goytía, *supra*, p. 134 *et seq.* Also art. by Morton C. Steinberg, "Sea Level Canal a Vital Defense Need," *Philadelphia Sunday Inquirer*, December 26, 1948; and by Sidney Shallet, "Can We Defend the Panama Canal?," *Saturday Evening Post*, October 9, 1948.

38. Scott Seegers, "The World's Best Business Set-Up," *supra*, and unsigned art., "Panamanian Bonds," *Inter-American Magazine*, May, 1944, p. 46.

39. Coördinator of Inter-American Affairs, *Basic Data on the Other American Republics* (Washington, 1944), p. 135.

40. República de Panamá, Ministro de Relaciones Exteriores, *Memoria 1943-1944* (Panamá, 1945), xxxiii.

41. M. de J. Quijano, *Una Campaña Antifascista, 1937-1940, op. cit.*, p. 3 of Preface.

42. Pan American Union, "The Americas and the War," *Bulletin of the Pan American Union,* LXXIX, July, 1945, p. 406.

43. Jesús Vázquez Gayoso, ed., *Una Nación en Guerra, supra,* p. 294.

CHAPTER NINE

The Pan American Movement Since 1944

BETWEEN THE CONFERENCE called to deal with the presenting of a united front to the Axis at Rio de Janeiro in January 1942, and that at Chapultepec in 1945, no other top-flight political meetings were held within the system of American states, and there was a conspicuous absence of Pan American activity as such. The nations of this hemisphere were mostly contributing on a much broader scope to the activities and purposes of the United Nations. Panama and the other Latin American states of course were present at important wartime meetings such as the Conferences on Food and Agriculture, and on Relief and Rehabilitation, in 1943, and the Monetary and Banking, and Aviation Conferences, in 1944, but these were not hemispheric, but world, convocations, and the American states participated in no sense as a regional bloc. The idea of regionalism seemed then to be submerged into a worldwide coöperation of all nations of good will. For this reason I have reserved discussion of Panama's part at these international wartime meetings for the following chapter dealing with the United Nations.

At Chapultepec, Mexico, in February and early March, 1945, the states of the Inter-American System, in their first important political gathering since the Rio meeting of 1942, discussed among other issues a proposal embodying

PAN AMERICAN MOVEMENT SINCE 1944   125

tentative plans for a permanent world organization, which had been issued by the Conference of the "Big Four" after the meetings at Dumbarton Oaks from August 21 to October 7, 1944. These proposals had recognized regional "agencies" and "arrangements." Consequently, Panama and her sister republics met at Chapultepec in the full desire and conviction that the Inter-American System continue to function as a regional organization and that their future role as members of any permanent world body would be fitted to that basic premise.

Panama's delegation to Chapultepec was headed by the Minister of Foreign Affairs, Roberto Jiménez, and included Jorge E. Boyd, Ricardo Marciacq, Juan Galindo, Miguel J. Moreno, Jr., and Armando Moreno G.[1] Señor Jiménez served as Panama's representative on the important Second Committee (World Organization),[2] and Señor Moreno, Second Secretary of the Ministry of Foreign Affairs, was elected Vice Chairman of the First Committee (Complementary Measures to Intensify the Coöperation in the War Effort).[3]

The two great issues of the Chapultepec meeting were the Dumbarton Oaks Proposals and the "Argentine Question." Latin American nations had not appreciated the exclusion of small powers from the Dumbarton Oaks Conference, and a region which had long worked to check great-power domination over its own affairs now viewed with alarm a prospective new world order which threatened to be based upon that very principle. Uruguay, Venezuela, Mexico, and Brazil had voiced criticisms of the Proposals long before the opening of the Chapultepec Conference.[4] The upshot of this was that there was strong support at the Mexico Meeting for a collective American attempt at the forthcoming San Francisco Conference to sponsor amendments to the Dumbarton Oaks Proposals which would accomplish the following objectives *vis-à-vis* the new World Organization:[5]

1. A clarification and definitive limitation of powers to be exercised by the world organization.

2. Larger representation for Latin American states and other small powers on the Security Council.

3. A full concession to the Inter-American System of authority to settle its own regional disputes.

Panama and several other Latin American states submitted *Observations Relative to the Dumbarton Oaks Proposals,* which generally covered the above points as basic alterations that they desired to have made in the Proposals. They resolutely supported the suggested changes through long debates and discussions in committees and upon the floor of the conference.[6]

The United States was understandably concerned at the headway made by this movement among the sister republics of the hemisphere. The United States sought to preserve the concept of the permanent United Nations essentially as the Dumbarton Oaks Proposals outlined it. At Chapultepec, therefore, the United States worked to turn aside, or at least to blunt, the Latin American effort to have the hemispheric bloc go to San Francisco committed to a struggle to alter the Proposals along the lines set forth above.[7] Since the Inter-American System had always operated on the basis of unanimous agreement, the refusal of the United States to go along meant that the resolution to sponsor "Hemispheric Amendments" at San Francisco could not be adopted. This did not settle the issue, however, but only meant that the battleground would shift, for most of the Latin American powers would go to San Francisco determined to there join with other small states in renewing the battle against "great power domination" of the world organization.

These developments demonstrate a very interesting attitude *vis-à-vis* the regional and the world organizations on the part of many leading citizens of Latin America, which contrast sharply with the view which they took in 1919 when the League of Nations was born. Then many of them believed that Latin America's experience in the regional organization had been, on the whole, an unsatisfactory one. They had felt all too often the overshadowing and overpowering presence and influence of the United States. They had turned eagerly to the League of Nations as the best possible counterpoise to the power of the United States.[8] But in 1945 the picture was radically altered. The long, hard struggle to bring the United States to full acceptance within the Americas of the principle of absolute nonintervention had been won at Buenos Aires in 1936. The Inter-American System, in 1945, therefore represented for these people the *summum bonum* in international organization,[9] since the juridical equality which its member states enjoyed was a blessing guaranteed against interference from the outside world by the power of the United States (exercised under what remained of the Monroe Doctrine) and against the traditional source of interference from within the hemisphere by the Protocol of Buenos Aires. Many Latin American statesmen consequently felt no imperative *personal* need for a world organization, and if one were to be formed which threatened the structure of their carefully constructed regional system they would be likely to be cold to it indeed. Since their states had been members of the wartime United Nations, they favored a peacetime U.N. largely for the good it was hoped it would do for the rest of the world.

In assessing the attitude of *Panama* upon this matter, however, I have considered that some divergence from the foregoing view can be found. Panama has as strong an attraction to the regional organization, and as determined a purpose to preserve it as any of her sister republics. But she has also sought in the new world organization a certain additional safeguard—frankly a counterpoise to the power of the United States. For the presence of the *Yanqui* Canal Zone across Panama has created issues between Panama and the United States since World War II which are peculiar in the Americas to these two powers alone, and quite alien to the relations between the United States and *any other* Latin American republic.[10] This point will be more fully dealt with in the succeeding chapter.

At the 1945 conference in Mexico the famous Act of Chapultepec was adopted, writing a new principle into the theory of collective American security.[11] The Declaration of Lima and its subsequent implementations at Panama, Havana, and Rio de Janeiro had all been concerned with collective action by the American states to meet a threat from *outside* the Hemisphere.[12] By this Act the use of sanctions was provided to prevent an aggression by one American state against another for the duration of the current war, with a recommendation for adoption of some similar permanent arrangement as soon as possible after the war.[13]

The development of this new principle had been in part occasioned by the wartime antics of Argentina. That republic had long clung to diplomatic ties with the Axis and had finally broken them under almost unprecedented pressures from sister American republics and Argentina's great economic partner and customer—Britain. But she still refused to declare war upon the Axis powers, and the rise of the Farrell-Perón leadership had alarmed all democratically inclined states as to her future intentions in the Americas. She had therefore not been invited to Chapultepec, since that conference was stated to be for consultation on problems of war and peace by America's belligerent powers.[14] Furthermore, as things stood, Argentina would have no chance to gain a seat at the forthcoming San Francisco Conference either, since the call for that had been limited to belligerents signatory to the United Nations Declaration of 1942.

All of the American states appreciated the fact that their prestige as a regional bloc of sister republics at San Francisco would be seriously impaired by the absence of a nation as important to the Western Hemisphere as the Argentine Republic. All of them had long cherished the principle of settlement of differences *within* their system—exclusion of an offender had never been regarded as a proper settlement by the American states—and finally, the Latin American nations felt they would need Argentina's vote in the battle to be waged at San Francisco against the theory of great power domination in the world organization. For these reasons, therefore, all of the Chapultepec conferees were most anxious that the Inter-American System should "close ranks," and that Argentina should join with them in presenting a solid American front.[15] It was in this spirit then that they formally invited Argentina to adhere to the Act of Chapultepec and to make herself eligible for a seat at San Francisco by declaring war upon the Axis[16]—an invitation which the rulers at Buenos Aires were constrained to accept with alacrity, since the military picture in Europe indicated that the Axis cause was doomed and that nothing could be gained by continuing the state of neutrality toward it.[17]

At Chapultepec the Panamanian delegation was very active in the routine work of the Conference. The Republic sponsored one project, the Convocation and Organization of Inter-American Conferences, which was considered by the Third Committee (on the Inter-

American System). It dealt with the five-year interval conferences and also proposed that the practice of holding consultative meetings of the Foreign Ministers be continued, with meetings to be called whenever the majority of governments should approve a request for one. This project was withdrawn from consideration before the committee took final action regarding it. However, the Conference did reorganize the Pan American Union to provide that special delegates from each state, instead of their diplomats at Washington, comprise the governing board of the Union. This was a change which had long been favored by many to end North American domination of the machinery of the regional system.[18]

Another Panamanian offering was a project for reduction of maritime freight rates, which was considered by the Fourth Committee (post-war economic and social problems), and was substantially accepted and included in a final resolution of the conference, which was a synthesis of a number of proposals dealing with transportation.[19]

This Fourth Committee considered a number of important matters. United States assurances of economic aid during the post-war transition period had been stated in far too generalized terms to satisfy many Latin American states frankly worried over the inevitable dislocations which the end of hostilities would bring.[20] There was much talk at Chapultepec of attempting to create some sort of an exclusive regional economy, and the Conference did decide to make permanent the Inter-American Financial and Economic Advisory Committee.[21]

An Economic Charter of the Americas was also promulgated whereby the American republics proclaimed their support of the free enterprise system and private ownership, and pledged themselves to act individually and jointly with each other to assure just and equitable treatment and encouragement for international businessmen and their enterprises, and to promote the flow of capital, technology, and trained personnel between states of the Americas by removing trade barriers and relaxing travel regulations.[22] This pledge was considerably weakened, however, by a failure to make specific commitments for lowering of international trade barriers. The United States had come to Chapultepec championing the effort to spell out such measures in terms of definitive commitments, but a protectionist bloc led by Carlos Lleras Restrepo, of Colombia, fought successfully to modify these undertakings to the point where they amounted merely to the foregoing pledge of pious intentions.[23] The consideration of economic questions at Chapultepec did, however, form a sort of preview of the agenda to be taken up by the Inter-American Technical Economic Conference, which was at that time scheduled to meet later in the same year.

In August and September of 1947 another special Inter-American Conference opened at Quitandinha Palace, the beautiful former summer residence of the Emperors of Brazil, located at Petropolis in the mountains, a short distance from Rio de Janeiro. This Conference had been convoked for the stated purpose of "maintenance of continental peace and security." The meeting was called in accordance with Part II of the Act of Chapultepec, which recommended the conclusion of a treaty after the war which would give permanent form to the Act's arrangement for American collective security during the remainder of the Second World War. Panama played a very important role at this conference. She was one of eight states submitting drafts of a tentative treaty for making permanent the arrangements of Chapultepec. The distinguished Ricardo J. Alfaro headed his country's delegation to this conference. Other Panamanian delegates were José Edgardo Lefevre, Abdiel José Arias, and José Guillermo Batalla.[24]

Dr. Alfaro served as chairman of Committee II (dealing with measures to be taken in case of threats or acts of aggression), and the official report of that committee to the Conference spoke of the "wise, intelligent direction of one of America's outstanding men, Dr. Ricardo J. Alfaro."[25] Señor Lefevre was a member of the Second Sub-Committee of Committee I (Protocolary Articles),[26] and Dr. Alfaro was also one of the vice-presidents of the Conference.

Except for the Consultative Meeting of the Foreign Ministers in 1939, at which she was the host state, I consider that Panama at Petropolis enjoyed a more prominent position, and made more important contributions, than in any Pan American meeting in which the Republic has been represented up to the time of this writing.

The Panamanian draft differed at the outset from that submitted by the United States. The old Latin American insistence on the statement of defined Rights and Duties of States contrasted with the omission of any reference to the subject in the *Yanqui* proposition. The drafts of Colombia, Ecuador, and Mexico reiterated Panama's position, but the conference omitted the matter from the final text, accepting the North American argument that the ninth international meeting of the American states, forthcoming at Bogotá, was scheduled to take up the drafting of such a statement of principles.[27]

With respect to the question of just what sort of circumstances would bring the collective defense machinery of the Americas into operation Panama went beyond most of the states in referring not only to "acts or threats of aggression" but also to a "conflict which may threaten or endanger the peace of the continent." The conference accepted this wording.²⁸ Panama joined with Brazil in including the "right of passage" among the specific measures to be agreed upon at the consultative meeting which would be called in the event of a threat to hemispheric peace. The Conference decided to leave the issue of specific methods go over to Bogotá.

During consideration of the nature of the Consultative Organ, the mechanism for implementing treaty arrangements, Panama proposed the creation of a special organ to exercise all political functions.²⁹ The other drafts either gave this job to the Pan American Union Governing Board, or left the choice of mechanism or agency to the parties in each instance. The conference decided that the Foreign Ministers should make up the Organ of Consultation. Panama joined with Ecuador and the United States in proposing that agreement on collective measures should be reached by a two-thirds vote. The Conference decided that initiation of consultation should be by a majority; all other decisions by a two-thirds vote; and with all parties bound to accept the decision except that no state would be required to use force without its consent.³⁰

With respect to relations between the Pan American Defense Union and the United Nations, and the question of consistency with the United Nations Charter, the proposals made in the Panamanian draft were substantially accepted at Petropolis. The problem of continuing the Inter-American System without it conflicting with the machinery and the purposes of the United Nations had been a matter of serious concern. The idea that regional security arrangements should only supplement and buttress, and ever be subordinate to the world organization, was piously expressed in the preamble of the Quitandinha Treaty, and a clause was included which declared that no provision of the treaty should be "construed as impairing the rights and obligations of the High Contracting Parties under the Charter of the United Nations."[31]

In preparing the Protocolary Articles the Panamanians pressed and won a very significant point. The drafting subcommittee had initially proposed an article providing for unlimited duration of the treaty. This would have represented a departure from the usual practice in past international defense accords. Panama sought to permit denunciation by individual states. Mexico and the United States also had supported this view in their proposed drafts. The final text accepted by the Conference declared that while the Treaty was to remain in force indefinitely, an individual state would be able to renounce it by giving written notice, and its denunciation would become effective two years after such notice.[32]

The Ninth International Conference of American States was held at Bogotá, Colombia, from March 30 to May 2, 1948. Here, as at Petropolis, Panama was represented by a large and distinguished delegation, headed by Mario de Diego, the Republic's Minister of Foreign Relations. Dr. Alfaro again was present to give the immense benefits of his long experience in international relations, and Roberto Jiménez, Eduardo A. Chiari, Pedro Moreno Correa, Emilio Clare, Enrique Narciso Garay, and Gabriel Hernández Méndez were the other members of the delegation.[33] Dr. Alfaro served as Vice Chairman of the vital First Committee (on the Organic Pact), and Enrique Narciso Garay was the Reporter of Sub-Committee Four-A (on preamble, the settlement of economic disputes, principles, transitory provision, and ratification and entry into force). Other Panamanian delegates served on the following committees: The Steering Committee, Coördination Committee, and groups working on Preamble, Rights and Duties of States, Specialized Organizations, Maritime

Transportation, Inter-American Travel, Social Guarantees, Coördination with U.N. Economic Organizations, Women's Rights and the Commission of Women, and Recognition of de Facto Governments and Maintenance of Democracy in America.[34]

As it had done at Petropolis and in meetings preliminary to the Bogotá Conference, Panama pressed for creation of a special "Council of Solidarity" with headquarters outside the United States to handle all political powers of the Inter-American System and withhold such functions from the Governing Board at Washington. Under the formula finally adopted the Governing Board was separated from the Pan American Union and renamed "The Council of the Organization of American States." The prohibition adopted at Chapultepec in 1945 against any member state designating its accredited diplomatic representative at Washington as its member of the Board was now relaxed and the designation of either such diplomat, or a special representative, to the new Council was made optional. It was provided that the Council should serve as a provisional Consultative Organ in cases under the Rio Treaty, but in any case of armed attack the Meeting of Foreign Ministers was to be convoked without delay and to supersede the Council.[35]

In addition to the Council and the Meeting of Foreign Ministers, the formal Charter of the Organization of American States adopted at Bogotá provided that the regular five-year meetings, now called "Inter-American Conferences," should be the supreme organ of the Organization. The specialized agencies and conferences were also to be continued and further developed, and the Pan American Union would function as the general secretariat of the Organization. The Inter-American Economic and Social Council, the Inter-American Council of Jurists, and the Inter-American Cultural Council were to function under the general cognizance of the Council of the Organization of American States. The Advisory Defense Committee was to be a direct agency of the Organ of Consultation (the Meeting of Foreign Ministers or, provisionally, the Council) set up at Rio.[36]

The Conference also adopted, in addition to the permanent Charter, a pact for economic coöperation,[37] a resolution declaring that all totalitarianism, and particularly communism, is repugnant to the American peoples, and a resolution calling for the peaceful ending of colonial rule by non-American powers in this hemisphere. There was also some talk of the Rodriguez Larreta Doctrine at Bogotá. This formula had been advanced in 1945 by a Uruguayan statesman and proposed the use of moral intervention by withholding diplomatic recognition from *de facto* governments regarded as repugnant to Pan American ideologies of orderly self government under law.[38] Panama's senior statesman, Ricardo J. Alfaro, has long been an advocate of the Rodriguez Larreta Doctrine, and would have been pleased to see it formally accepted at Bogotá, but it mustered little support outside the delegations of Panama and Uruguay.

The Larreta Doctrine had been put forth as a contrasting viewpoint to that propounded in the Estrada Doctrine, which the Government of Ecuador had brought forth also in 1945, and which called for unbroken continuity of diplomatic relations even when changes in government were brought about by revolution in defiance of democratic principles and practices. The Estrada Doctrine had formed the basis of a study of the problem of recognizing *de facto* governments undertaken by the Inter-American Juridical Committee at the direction of the Chapultepec Conference. But the Juridical Committee had not completed its report and the Ecuadorian delegation had injected the issue into the Bogotá Conference by submitting the Estrada Doctrine again as a formal project. Uruguay had then countered by proposing the Rodriguez Larreta Doctrine.

Both of these doctrines represented extreme viewpoints.[39] Resolution XXXV, the final act of the Bogotá Conference on this point, constituted a compromise along the lines of a resolution put forward by the United States and favored by a large majority of the delegations, who felt that both the Estrada and Larreta doctrines would have deprived each state of the sovereign right to decide for itself whether or not to maintain diplomatic relations with another government. Resolution XXXV states the general desirability of continuity in diplomatic relations among the American states without committing them to establish or reject relations with any new revolutionary regime. The resolution also declared that recognition should not in future be construed to amount to approval or disapproval of the internal policies of any American government.[40]

In the time which has elapsed since the Bogotá Conference a number of "constitutional" governments have been overthrown by violence, including that of Panama in the Arnulfo Arias coup of December, 1949. It has been argued by the proponents of the Larreta Doctrine that Resolution XXXV may have helped encourage these forceful overturns by favoring establishment of diplomatic relations with revolutionary *de facto* regimes. Resolution XXXV has not finally settled the issue in any case. Inasmuch as the Inter-American Juridical Committee was not prepared to submit at Bogotá the report on *de facto* governments which the Chapultepec Conference had directed it to prepare, the Ninth Conference postponed final definitive action until the Tenth meeting should be held. The Larreta Doctrine will certainly be heard from again at that time. What Dr. Alfaro may have to say about it in the future will be of high interest in view of recent political happenings in Panama.

During the consideration of social and cultural matters the Panamanian delegation sponsored a resolution to acknowledge the valuable contributions of the International Red Cross and to support the activities of that organization. The Conference accepted this as Resolution XXV.[41] The Isthmian Republic, long active in promoting the Inter-American Commission of Women,[42] also supported a convention on granting of political rights to women, and a second convention granting women equal civil rights with men.[43] The Panamanian Constitution of 1946 had already incorporated both concepts into the basic law of the Republic.[44]

During the course of the Bogotá meeting a fierce outbreak of rioting swept the city, apparently touched off by the assassination of the leader of the leftist Colombian Liberals, Gaitán. The people of Panama, like those of the other American states, were gravely concerned at the news of this outbreak, for it completely disrupted the proceedings of the Conference for five days, and in the turbulence and bloodshed, which took over 1,200 lives before troops quelled the uprising, the distinguished foreigners in Bogotá were by no means assured of personal safety. There were elements in Panama, however, that were slow to accept at full face value the declarations of the Colombian Conservative Government and the United States Secretary of State, that the demonstration had been set off by remote control from Moscow.[45] From this distance it seems they may very well have been right, and that it was mainly a forlorn attempt of the once-great Colombian Liberals to parade their woes before a distinguished audience of hemispheric statesmen. The spectacle of the semi-Fascist, Laureano Gómez, presiding over the opening session of the Conference could very logically have been much more of a spark to arouse the followers of Gaitán than any instructions issuing out of the Soviet's agents in Colombia.

Through the years of the Second World War, and after, the Republic of Panama continued to give support to the various specialized agencies of the Inter-American System. In April of 1944 Senorita Anita Ramírez Duque represented her country at the largest and most successful meeting yet of the Inter-American Commission of Women;[46] Galileo Patiño served as chairman of the Fifth Committee (on Libraries) at the Assembly of Librarians of the Americas in Washington in May of 1947;[47] in August, 1947 the City of Panama was host to the Inter-American Congress of Directors of Tourism and Immigration;[48] the Republic's coöperation in pushing the Inter-American Highway toward completion all but eliminated one of the greatest obstacles in the path of that goal by bringing the road through the jungles north of David to just twenty-five miles from the Costa Rican border.[49] A number of distinguished Isthmian lawyers attended the Sixth Conference of the Inter-American Bar Association in Detroit, Michigan, May 22 to June 1, 1949, which was opened with a message from President Truman.[50] Other professional leaders have represented the Republic at many similar Pan American gatherings, which have been held with increasing frequency since the end of the war has eased travel difficulties within the hemisphere.[51] Cultural interchanges have also greatly aided the spirit of Inter-American coöperation.[52] A noteworthy example of this was a Carnegie Foundation Research grant in 1948 to Professor John Biesanz of Tulane University to undertake a sociological study of Panama. Professor Biesanz had served as visiting Professor of Sociology at the University of Panama in 1946 and 1947.[53] In every conceivable way the Panamanian people have earnestly coöperated and worked to make the Pan American movement the successful regional organization which it is today—a success which has undoubtedly inspired, at least in part, the creation of the Western European bloc as a project in collective international coöperation. In the mid-twentieth century, when the regional organization seems to be the most valued vehicle of collective security, the Inter-American System has pointed the way.

Footnotes

CHAPTER NINE

The Pan American Movement Since 1944

1. U.S. State Department, *Report of the U.S. Delegation to the Inter-American Conference on Problems of War and Peace at Mexico City, February 21—March 8, 1945* (Washington, 1946), p. 40.
2. *Ibid.*, p. 55.
3. *Ibid.*, p. 9.
4. *New York Times*, October 31, 1944 and November 2, 1944, reporting views of U.S. Secretary of State Edward R. Stettinius on the Dumbarton Oaks Proposal vis-à-vis the American nations.
5. Arthur P. Whitaker, ed., *Inter-American Affairs 1945, Annual Survey No. 5*, pp. 10, 50-51, 67-71.
6. República de Panamá, Ministro de Relaciones Exteriores, *Memoria 1943-1944* (Panamá, 1945), p. xlvii. Also *Panama Star and Herald*, March 1-10, 1945; also, the *New York Times*, March 5-8, 1945.
7. Hon. Harley A. Notter, then an advisor on Latin America in the Office of Special Political Affairs, who accompanied the U.S. delegation to Chapultepec, expressed this as his *personal* and, of course, unofficial view of what occurred, in an interview with this writer, April 8, 1950.

8. George H. Blakeslee, *The Recent Foreign Policy of the United States* (New York 1925), pp. 174-75, states ". . . some Latin Americans are saying that they have already been given more genuine recognition and accorded more actual power as fully coequal states in the League of Nations than they have received in their own Pan American Union . . ." Samuel F. Bemis, *Latin American Policy of the United States, op. cit.*, speaking of Argentine opinion said "many . . . mistrusted and resented Pan Americanism and the Monroe Doctrine . . . and they began to look more and more to Geneva as a diplomatic lodestar." For Panamanian views on the League, see Chapter Five, pp. 53-55, *supra*.

9. P. H. Bidwell, "Good Neighbors in the War and After," art. in *Foreign Affairs*, XXI, April 1943, pp. 524-34. Also Ezéquiel Padilla, "The American System and the World Organization," *Foreign Affairs*, October 1945, pp. 99-107.

10. In this respect, Mr. Notter has also expressed a *personal* opinion in agreement with the writer. A very recent and striking example of Panama's views is seen in the offer at Lake Success of Carlos Brin, Chief of the Panamanian delegation to the United Nations Assembly, to give the *United Nations* the bases built in the Republic during World War II by the U.S.A. and since 1946 denied to further U.S. occupation. See *Panama Star and Herald*, August 3-5, 1950, and October 8, 1950; also, the *Chicago Daily News* and the *Washington Evening Star*, October 7, 1950, quoting Dr. Brin as emphasizing the purpose of the Panamanian government to contribute "gratis" to the U.N. for *collective security* the bases to which the U.S.A. was refused a remunerative leasehold after 1946. The attitude of Panama toward the United Nations was first strongly pubished in the Ministerio de Relaciones Exteriores, *Memoria 1943-1944* (Panamá, 1945), p. xlvii.

11. Ricardo J. Alfaro, "La Intervención colectiva de las repúblicas américanas," *Revista Derecho Internacional* (Havana, December 1945), pp. 153-62.

12. Dexter Perkins, *The United States and the Caribbean*, (Cambridge, Mass., 1947), pp. 225-26; and Arthur P. Whitaker, *The United States and South America, the Northern Republics* (Cambridge, Mass., 1948), pp. 142-44.

13. Charles G. Fenwick, "The American Republics and International Law," *Bulletin of the Pan American Union*, April 14, 1947. Also Laurence Duggan, *The Americas, the Search for Hemispheric Security* (New York, 1949), p. 113.

14. U.S. State Department, *Consultation among the American Republics with Respect to the Argentine Situation*, Inter-American Series No. 29 (Washington, 1946), p. 129.

15. Laurence Duggan, *The Americas, etc., supra,* pp. 109-15.
16. U.S. State Department, *Report of the Delegation of the U.S.A. to the Inter-American Conference on Problems of War and Peace, Mexico City, Mexico, February 21—March 8, 1945* (Washington, 1946), p. 133.
17. *New York Times,* March 28, 1945.
18. U.S. State Department, *Report of the U.S. Delegation to Mexico City, supra,* pp. 16-27.
19. *Ibid.,* p. 27.
20. Mary W. Williams, *The People and Politics of Latin America,* rev. ed. (Boston, 1945), p. 903.
21. Dana G. Munro, "The Mexico City Conference and the Inter-American System," *U.S. Department of State Bulletin,* XII, April 8, 1945.
22. National Foreign Trade Council, Inc., and Council for Inter-American Cooperation, pamphlet, *Economic Proposals for Consideration of Ninth International Conference of American States* (New York, 1947), p. 4.
23. A. P. Whitaker, *The United States and South America, etc., supra,* p. 1943.
24. U.S. State Department, *Report of the Delegation of the U.S.A. to the Inter-American Conference for the Maintenance of Continental Peace and Security, Quitandinha, Brazil, August 15—September 2, 1947* (Washington, 1948), pp. 167-68. The delegation's staff included Renato Azores and Harmodio Arias, Jr., legal advisors; Luis Carlos Aleman and Antonio Zubieta, economic advisors; Roque Javier Laurenza, Secretary; and Gerardo Díaz L. and Eusebio A. Gonzalez, Aides.
25. *Ibid.,* p. 141.
26. *Ibid.,* p. 140.
27. *Ibid.,* pp. 13 and 73.
28. *Ibid.,* pp. 24, 25, 100, and 101.
29. *Ibid.,* pp. 26, 27, and 183-84.
30. *Ibid.,* p. 28. See also U.S. Department of States, *Press Release No. 1025,* December 27, 1948; also, State Department *Bulletin,* February 8, 1948.
31. U.S. State Department, *Report of the U.S. Delegation at Quitandinha, supra,* pp. 31-36, 121, and 173.
32. *Ibid.,* pp. 37-38, 127.
33. U.S. Department of State, *Report of the Delegation of the U.S., Ninth International Conference of American States, Bogotá, Colombia, March 30—May 2, 1948* (Washington, 1948), pp. 285-86.
34. *Ibid.,* pp. 304-8.
35. *Ibid.,* pp. 19-22. See also Alberto Lleras, "The Bogotá Conference," *Bulletin of the Pan American Union,* Vol. 82, August

1948; and U.S. Department of State, *Press Release 400,* May 21, 1948, "The Final Act of Bogotá."

36. William Sanders, "Bogotá Conference," art. in *International Conciliation,* June 1948.

37. James W. Gantenbein, *The Evolution of our Latin American Policy, A Documentary Record* (New York, 1950), p. 268.

38. Charles G. Fenwick, "The Recognition of De Facto Governments," *American Journal of International Law,* October 1948, p. 865.

39. Charles G. Fenwick, "Pact of Bogotá and Other Juridical Decisions of the Ninth Conference," *Bulletin of the Pan American Union,* Vol. 82, August 1948. Also see Laurence Duggan, *The Americas,* etc., *supra,* pp. 199-201.

40. U.S. State Department, Division of Publications, Office of Public Affairs, published release of June 8, 1949, *Relations with De Facto Governments in the American Republics;* also *Report of the U.S. Delegation . . . at Bogotá, supra,* pp. 82-83; also Duggan, *The Americas, supra,* p. 200.

41. U.S. State Department, *Report of the U.S. Delegation . . . at Bogotá, supra,* p. 89.

42. República de Panamá, Ministro de Relaciones Exteriores, *Memoria 1943-1944* (Panamá, 1945), p. lxi.

43. *Report of the U.S. Delegation at Bogotá, supra,* p. 91.

44. Russell H. Fitzgibbon, ed., *The Constitutions of the Americas as of January 1, 1948* (Chicago, 1948), pp. 608, citing Title III, Chap. I, Article 21; and 619, citing Title IV, Chap. I, Article 97. See also Austin F. MacDonald, *Latin American Politics and Government* (New York, 1949), p. 618.

45. *Panama Star and Herald,* April 10-15, 1948.

46. *The Inter-American Magazine,* June 1944, p. 29.

47. U.S. Department of State, *Program of the Interdepartmental Committee on Scientific and Cultural Cooperation,* reprint from State Department Bulletin (Washington, 1947), p. 12.

48. Pan American Union, *Inter-American Conferences, 1826-1948,* Congress and Conference Series No. 56 (Washington, 1949), p. 15.

49. *The Inter-American Magazine,* August 1946, p. 26.

50. *Journal of the American Judicature Society,* Vol. 32, No. 6 (Ann Arbor, Mich., 1949), p. 165.

51. For full lists, to 1949, *see* Pan American Union compilation, Note 48, *supra.*

52. U.S. Department of State, *Interdepartmental Committee on Cultural and Scientific Cooperation,* Inter-American Series No. 25, rev. (Washington, 1945), p. 1.

53. *Hispanic American Review,* May 1948, p. 313.

CHAPTER TEN

Panama and the United Nations

ON JANUARY 2, 1942, at the White House in Washington, D. C., the Republic of Panama joined with twenty-five other nations at war with the Axis in signing a formal pledge not to make a separate peace or armistice with the enemy, and declaring their aims to be "complete victory" over "savage and brutal forces seeking to subjugate the world."[1] This ceremony marked the birth of the United Nations. Originally the name designated the combination of powers allied to defeat the Axis in the Second World War, but as the conflict progressed and the certainty of ultimate victory grew there developed the further concept that the wartime "United Nations" could and should be continued after hostilities ceased as a permanent international organization to preserve the peace thus won.

As plans for this general international organization were being formulated there was much conjecture as to the relationship which the American republics and their regional system would bear to such a body.[2] At various wartime conferences Panama and the other Latin American states present in no sense participated as a collective Latin American bloc. The vital issue was the speedy winning of the war. A world-wide coalition had dedicated itself to the attainment of that goal. Any ideas of regionalism seemed to have been definitely submerged into a global coöperation of all nations of good will.

The first important general Allied conference was the United Nations Conference on Food and Agriculture held at Hot Springs, Virginia, in May 1943.[3] Out of this was organized the United Nations Food and Agriculture Organization. Panama's delegation included Ramón Antonio Vega, Eduardo Icaza, and Mario Guardia.[4] All belligerent Latin American powers were present at this meeting and, as one of the world's great food producing areas, were of prime importance in United Nations plans for mobilizing agricultural resources to help win the war.

In October 1943, the United Nations Relief and Rehabilitation Administration held its conference at Atlantic City, New Jersey.[5] Panama's delegates here were Enrique A. Jiménez, Ricardo A. Morales, and Licenciado Narciso E. Garay.[6] Here plans were laid for war relief operations in Europe and Asia. The Relief and Rehabilitation Administration (UNRRA) was created as a continuing organization and may be regarded as a sort of forerunner of a permanent general world body.

In July of 1944 the United Nations Monetary and Banking Conference was held at Bretton Woods. The Panamanian delegates were A. Guillermo Arango, and Licenciado Narciso E. Garay.[7] Panama was not so vitally concerned in this meeting as most other Latin American states, since the principal problem on the agenda was a system of controlling transactions in foreign exchange. This question is, and has been, academic for all practical purposes in Panama, because the Panamanian dollar (the *balboa*) is firmly pegged to the United States dollar, cent for cent,[8] and the isthmian republic automatically enjoys the benefits of a favorable position held by the United States in foreign exchange. The Bretton Woods Conference created the International Bank for Reconstruction and Development, to assist in reconstruction, promote private foreign investments by means of guarantees, and boost international trade.[9]

Another conference which was of far more concern to Panama was the International Civil Aviation Conference held at Chicago, Illinois, from November 1st through December 7th, 1944. The Republic was represented at this meeting by Carlos Icaza, Chairman of the Delegation, Inocencio Galindo, Enrique Lefevre, and Licenciado Narciso Garay.[10] The Isthmian state served with Australia, Egypt, Greece, and Norway upon the Credentials Committee.[11]

Latin American nations did not play a leading role in this conference since the great air powers such as Britain and the United States carried the most influence, but the Latin American states did very frequently act in concert during the proceedings. This appearance of a "Latin American bloc" excited considerable comment, for it was the first time these republics had ever achieved such solidarity upon the stage of international affairs. The United States had recently appeared to many Latin Americans to be cultivating great-power relations at the expense of Inter-American relations, and this "bloc" was the natural result of the smaller states of the hemisphere feeling a need to draw closer to one another for mutual protection against possible pressure upon them from the great powers.[12] In this conference the Latin American bloc opposed the establishment generally of strong international controls over aviation. Panama was one of the most vocal of the Latin American bloc, and since the Isthmus was by the bare fact of geography of immense importance to air routes, the voice of Panama was heard with attention. Not only did Panama take her place in the regional Latin

American group, but she was also to be found along with Peru, Bolivia, Ecuador, Colombia, and Venezuela on certain issues of special concern to that "Bolivarian" group.

Carlos Icaza addressed the Conference saying that the Republic of Panama "opposed establishing an International Board with authority to permit or control flights over its territory." The Panamanians declared that even though international agreements might contain language "designed" to "protect" small powers, such nations had a fundamental right as sovereign entities to take their own risks and assume the consequences of so doing. Other small nations seconded these declarations.[13] A number of amendments sponsored by Panama and the others of the "small power" category were adopted: conserving of sovereign rights in airspaces, rights to control routings and franchises, training and competency of pilots, and ownership of aircraft by nationals.[14]

The Republic was particularly concerned with international air traffic between various points in Northern South America, the Caribbean Islands, Central America, and the southern United States, for it expected to be a key stopover point on such flights.[15] The Conference adjourned on December 7, 1944, after creating a Provisional International Civil Aviation Organization which would have a twenty-member council. The functions of this body were principally to be to attempt to arbitrate disputes among the powers signatory to the convention creating it. Another action of the Conference of interest to our subject was a convention agreeing upon nationality markings of aircraft. The Republic of Panama designation was to be "RX," and that of the United States "N."[16]

During the early autumn of this same year, 1944, the origins of a permanent United Nations structure were developed in a conference of the "Big Four" (Russia, Britain,

China, and the United States) at Dumbarton Oaks from August 21 to October 7. At this meeting were issued the formal "Proposals" which embodied tentative plans for a lasting world organization. Regional "agencies" and "arrangements" were recognized by Article VIII, Section C, of these Proposals. It was thus clearly contemplated that the American republics would in some degree, at least, continue to function as a Western Hemispheric organization.[17]

In February and early March, 1945, as detailed in the preceding chapter of this work, the states of the Inter-American System had convened at Chapultepec, Mexico, in the first important political conference of the hemispheric organization since the Rio gathering of the foreign ministers in January 1942. At Chapultepec the Dumbarton Oaks Proposals were discussed and debated at considerable length.

The American states made it plain that it would be their intent from 1945 onward to play a role in world international coöperation which would always be conditioned by influences from within their hemispheric organization. Although pledging their best efforts to attain the objectives fundamentally aspired to by "peoples everywhere," and declaring their purpose to coöperate with all "like-minded nations," and to conduct regional activities and procedures in consistency with "the purposes and principles of the general international organization when it shall be formed," the Latin American states did not by these piously phrased generalities obscure their determination to amend the Dumbarton Oaks Proposals along these general lines:

1. To clearly define and limit the powers of the projected world organization.

2. To secure larger representation for small powers gen-

erally, and Latin American powers specifically, upon the projected "Security Council."

3. To define a wide field of jurisdiction (including settlement of regional disputes) to agencies such as the Inter-American System.[18]

The refusal of the United States to go along had prevented the Chapultepec Conference from formally recommending that the American states sponsor such amendments to the Proposals. Traditionally the Inter-American System had adopted final acts only by unanimous concurrence of participating members. But lack of a formal recommendation did not prevent the Latin American nations from carrying their fight independently to the San Francisco Conference of the United Nations for International Organization, which convened from April 25 to May 28, 1945 to formally inaugurate the permanent United Nations and promulgate its Charter of Organization.

Membership in the San Francisco Conference was at first limited to those states which had declared war on the Axis and adhered to the United Nations Declaration of January 2, 1942. The Republic of Panama of course met these qualifications and thus became a charter member of the permanent United Nations organization. The Isthmian Republic was represented at San Francisco by Roberto Jiménez, Ricardo J. Alfaro, Octavio Méndez Pereira, Juan R. Morales, and Abdiel J. Arias. Dr. Jiménez served as a member of the Preparatory Commission.[19]

The Act of Chapultepec and the "Argentine Question" were major issues of the Conference with entirely American backgrounds, but most of the Latin American powers were equally interested in the question of the *liberum veto,* which the European War Allies (the so-called "Big Three" —Russia, Britain, and the United States) had decided at

Yalta to demand for themselves on the Security Council.[20]

Although their battle against the veto won support from small nations located in other parts of the world, the Latin American states suffered defeat upon this issue. One factor of great importance to this outcome was the adamant position of the United States alongside the other great powers in support of the veto power.[21]

In spite of the fact that Argentina had responded to the invitation of the Mexico City Conference, had declared war on Germany on March 27, 1945, and had signed the Act of Chapultepec, the Soviet Foreign Minister, M. Molotov, steadfastly opposed the admission of Argentina to the San Francisco Conference. The United States had indicated its satisfaction with the "new" Argentina in a radio speech of Nelson Rockefeller.[22] The issue was one which could be determined by majority vote, and the American states voted as a solid bloc, making up two-thirds of the majority of nations which voted the admission of the Argentine Republic.[23] This represented a signal triumph for both the American regional concept of a "united front" and for Latin America, albeit several of the American states felt that the record of Argentina during the Second World War constituted nothing which could be viewed with pride.[24] Panama was among these, and their collective "conscience" was somewhat appeased by following Mexico's lead in the successful fight to exclude Franco Spain. The Latin American bloc also sponsored a Statement of Principles and Purposes of the United Nations Organization, a Definition of Powers, and a Declaration for the International Protection of Human Rights, which were accepted in the final Act. All of these helped to clarify hazy phraseology of the Dumbarton Oaks Proposals.[25]

The Act of Chapultepec precipitated a major controversy at San Francisco. The question was raised as to whether the Security Council should not first delegate specific authority to the Inter-American System before the Chapultepec procedure could properly be put into effect and the American nations take action as a regional organ to repel an aggression by one American state against another. Article 51 of the United Nations Charter finally recognized the right of "collective" resistance to "armed attack." This of course did not go as far as the Act of Chapultepec, which also contemplated possible collective action to *prevent* an attack.[26]

On November 13, 1945, the Republic of Panama deposited her ratification of the Charter adopted at the San Francisco Conference.[27] The Isthmian state was thus present when the first General Assembly of the United Nations convened at London, January 10, 1946.[28] Although each member state has but one vote in the Assembly, it may be represented by as many as five delegates. Panama was represented at London by Roberto Jiménez and Demetrio A. Porras. Señor Jiménez was the first Panamanian to be honored with a high office in the world organization, serving as Chairman of the Sixth (Legal) Committee of the first and second parts of the First Regular Session of the General Assembly. Mario de Diego, Jorge E. Boyd, Germán Gil Guardia, Octavio Méndez Pereira, Hernan Porras, and Arturo de la Guardia are other citizens of the Republic who have served as delegates to the General Assembly during various periods of the First Session.[29]

Panama has thrice drawn attention by its activity with respect to important controversial issues before the world organization. The first such occasion was when the colonial powers of the world, acting in accordance with Chapter XI of the United Nations Charter dealing with "non-self governing peoples," submitted lists of the regions under their respective flags which they considered to be in such a category, and therefore subject to United Nations provisions for trusteeship territories.

The United States included the Panama Canal Zone in its list of such areas,[30] and the Panamanian delegation immediately raised a vigorous protest, issuing an official declaration maintaining that the inclusion of the Canal Zone among the "non-self governing" territories mentioned in Article 73(e) of the Charter must be regarded as an error, since *sovereignty* over the Canal Zone "had never been transferred to the United States."[31]

This action once again brought to the fore a long smouldering issue. As we have had occasion to note before the Hay-Bunau-Varilla Treaty had granted to the United States "all the rights, power, and authority" which it "would possess and exercise if it were sovereign—to the entire exclusion of the exercise by the Republic of Panama of any such rights, power, or authority." Not only was this issue paraded in the old days before the League of Nations[32] and in the literature produced by some of Panama's most respected scholars,[33] but at times it had even been the crux of litigation before the Supreme Court and other United States judicial tribunals.[34] No clear-cut judicial determination has yet been made by a competent court of last resort.

The executive branch of the North American Government has always conducted itself in accord with the principle that the United States was in a position *equivalent* to sovereignty.[35] Certainly the United States exercises sufficient *majestas* under the 1903 Treaty to be utterly exclusive of any claim of Panama to exercise possessory rights. In such circumstances the theoretical "sovereign title" becomes rather empty. The United States seemed to consider that its *exercise* of sovereign right brings the Canal Zone within the purview of the U.N. Charter clauses dealing with Trusteeship Territories. The listing of such territories had to be a unilateral action of the reporting power. This principle has been determined by the Special Committee of the Fourth Committee of the General Assembly, which was created by Resolution 146 (II) of November 3, 1947 to examine the information transmitted by the colonizing powers under Article 73(e) of the Charter.

During meetings of this Committee in September, 1948, held in Paris, a case similar to Panama's claims anent the Canal Zone arose. The Soviet representative attempted to persuade the committee not to consider information relating to Indonesia which had been presented by The Netherlands. It was stated on behalf of the Secretariat that the Secretary-General had no option but to summarize and analyze *any* information transmitted by the colonial powers. The Committee then decided by 8 votes for, 1 against, and 4 abstentions that the Soviet proposal was "beyond the competence of the Committee."[36] The Panama Canal Zone seems to be an analogous case, for the action of the Committee implies that determination of regions to be reported under Article 73(e) lies *exclusively* with the reporting power in the light of its constitutional relationships with the territories for whose administration it is responsible. Under the circumstances, therefore, the Panamanian protest amounted to nothing more than a reiteration, for the record, of Panama's historic claims over this issue. It is of interest to note, however, that on at least one occasion after the Panamanian protest the United States representative on this Special Committee *did* omit the Canal Zone from a list of "non-self governing" territories, which he submitted as part of a proposed "working paper."[37] Whether this is to be construed as a quiet acceptance by the United States of Panamanian sovereignty within the Canal Zone is highly conjectural in the opinion of this writer.

Another United Nations issue in which Panama was concerned was the elaborate report of the Special Committee on Palestine which was delivered to the General Assembly during the summer of 1947, three months after the Committee began its investigations in the Holy Land and Near East in May. Panama was a member of the United Nations Commission on Palestine then created, and Eduardo Morgan was the Republic's representative on the Commission.[38] Dr. Ralph Bunche, of the United States, was the Chairman of this body, after the assassination of Count Folke Bernadotte of Sweden. The painstaking and generally successful labors of the Commission earned the plaudits of the entire world at the time, although there has lately been a growing fear that its settlement of the Palestine question will prove to have not been a final one.

The other United Nations business in which Panama has played a leading role has been in the preparation of a Declaration on the Rights and Duties of States—long a favorite Latin American project. The eminent Panamanian statesman whose name has so often figured in this dissertation, Dr. Ricardo J. Alfaro, former President of the Republic, has from the very inception of the United Nations organization urged official action at various meetings to breathe new life into this idea. He had been hard at work upon a pronouncement along the lines of the Convention on the Rights and Duties of States adopted by the American republics at Montevideo in 1933. In the fall of 1946 this draft was sponsored by Panama in the General Assembly.

By Resolution 38 (I) of December 11, 1946 the General Assembly instructed the Secretary-General to transmit the

Alfaro Declaration to all member states and to bodies concerned with international law for their comments and observations. The General Assembly also referred the Declaration to its Committee on the Progressive Development of International Law and its Codification. That Committee recommended postponement of consideration of the subject and reference to the newly created International Law Commission.[39]

Upon this recommendation by the Sixth Committee, the General Assembly voted 39-0 that the Commission should use the Alfaro Draft submitted by Panama as the basis of its study. This vote came after an amendment sponsored by Soviet Russia to delete any reference to the Draft Declaration proposed by Panama was beaten by a vote of 30 to 5. Thus in 1949 Dr. Alfaro had the satisfaction of seeing his Declaration taken up for consideration by the Commission on International Law, of which he was a member. The Commission met at Lake Success from April 12 to June 9, 1949, under the chairmanship of Judge Manley O. Hudson of the United States.[40]

The Commission considered the Panamanian draft in three readings. Although changes were made in language and arrangement, the Draft Declaration on Rights and Duties of States which the Commission finally approved and voted to submit directly to the General Assembly was in substance the Panamanian draft. The Declaration contains four basic rights and ten fundamental duties.[41] It recognized the rights of (1) independence, (2) self defense, (3) equality of states, and (4) territorial jurisdiction. The duties are (1) non-intervention, (2) refraining from fomenting civil strife, (3) respect for human rights, (4) maintenance of national order, (5) settlement of disputes by peaceful means, (6) refraining from the use of force against other states, (7) declining assistance to a state engaged in illegal use of force, (8) refusing to recognize territorial acquisitions obtained by unlawful means, (9) carrying out obligations in good faith, and (10) conducting international relations in accordance with the principle that international law has supremacy over the sovereignty of any individual state.

Two members of the Commission, Vladimir M. Koretsky of the Soviet Union, and Manley O. Hudson of the United States, voted against the Declaration.[42] Koretsky declared that the Panamanian proposal could be distorted into a "super state" exploitation of the world in complete derogation of the ideal of juridical equality of states, and he objected that the draft which was finally approved went even beyond the Panamanian draft in denying the sovereignty of states. Hudson stated that he opposed the draft because it "went beyond the Charter of the United Nations and beyond international law at its present stage of development."

With the opposition of the United States and Russia thus assured it was certain that the Draft Declaration would encounter rough going in the General Assembly. On October 16, 1949, the Sixth Committee presented to the Assembly a resolution sponsored by Argentina, The Netherlands, and the United States. This resolution states that the General Assembly has encountered some difficulties in formulating basic rights and duties of states "in the light of new developments of international law and in harmony with the Charter of the United Nations and the need for continuing study with regard to this subject." It recalls that it is a responsibility of the U.N., and more specifically of the General Assembly, to encourage the progressive development of international law, and its codification. It then declares that the Draft Declaration is to be transmitted to member states and they are requested to furnish comments and suggestions by July 1, 1950 and to say (1) whether any further action should be taken by the General Assembly on the Draft Declaration, and (2) the exact nature of the document to be aimed at, if so. A text of the Draft Declaration was appended to the Resolution.[43]

After some debate the Assembly, on November 2, 1949, adopted this Resolution by a vote of 39 for, none against, and 10 abstentions.[44] As of the date of this writing in the late summer of 1950 the results of this poll of member states for comments and suggestions are not known. The past history of the effort to produce a Declaration on Rights and Duties of States, however, indicates little likelihood that any agreement can be reached in the present state of world antagonism. Dr. Alfaro is probably due for continued disappointment in his efforts to bring this matter to a successful conclusion.

The Panamanian Draft may possibly indicate an attitude on the part of the Isthmian Republic *vis-à-vis* the world organization and the position relative to it of the Inter-American System, which this writer believes has more and more tended to diverge from that common to the majority of Latin American states. As noted elsewhere in this work, Latin America generally underwent a change from the old effort to find in a world organization an order that would be paramount to a regional system which all too often had fallen under the dominating influences of the United States. This change was apparent at Chapultepec, and even more so at San Francisco. The Latin American nations had then sought to preserve and strengthen their American regional organization even at the expense of the incipient world body. In these meetings Panama had gone along with her sister nations,[45] but I have the impression from conversations I have had with persons of all shades of political opinion upon the Isthmus that this course was undertaken with some hesitancy and even misgiving, and that after San Francisco the trend was all in favor of bolstering the supremacy of the United Nations over any regional system. The Alfaro draft incorporates such an idea and, significantly, met the opposition of both the United States and Argentina, two nations often at loggerheads within the Americas on other issues.

The causes for this are not difficult to ascertain. In the first place the presence of the *Yanqui* Canal Zone across her territory creates political, social, and economic problems for Panama *vis-à-vis* the United States which are entirely foreign to the present situation of any other Latin American state. The tremendous pressures of North American influences in almost every phase of Panamanian life cause the Republic's leaders, of virtually every party, to instinctively seek to find in the United Nations, as once they so futilely did in the League of Nations, a possible counterpoise to *Yanqui* power. They frankly do not regard the Inter-American System as the completely adequate answer because of the practical realities of their position. The controversy with the United States over the Defense Bases since 1945, considered in the next chapter, and the effects upon Panama's national economy of demobilization in the Canal Zone and the operation of the Government Commissaries there, have all been factors in very recent history which tended to confirm these attitudes. This writer has been impressed by the unanimity with which these views were expressed to him by members of otherwise hopelessly divided factions in Panama's torrid political scene. Such leaders as Enrique Jiménez, Ricardo Alfaro, Harmodio Arias, Daniel Chanis, and Arnulfo Arias can apparently meet on this ground, if no other, because it touches the very wellsprings of Panama's national pride.

Enrique A. Jiménez, who was President of the Republic in 1946 and 1947 when the defense bases issue almost drove the United States and Panama into complete estrangement, expresses this basic uncertainty of the Panamanian national sentiment in language which becomes quite significant when one couples the fact that he occupied the high office of chief executive of Panama with the fact that he also adhered to political factions which have generally been friendly toward the United States. His words are quite typical of sentiments expressed to this writer by many other lesser Panamanians.

... there has been ... a lack of understanding of the Panamanian people. ... The United States Government competes unfairly and unjustly ... with the industry and commerce of Panama. ... we ask ... that we be permitted to make our contribution with the dignity becoming a free, independent people, and ... consistent with our sovereignty. ... .[46]

Ex-President Jiménez then goes on to point out that Panamanians like peoples of most of the lesser states of the world have always been most jealous of this concept of "sovereign independence" and ever ready to guard it against even the indirect threat of economic penetration such as the competition of the Canal Zone Commissaries. It was natural for the Isthmian Republic to seek in the new world organization a bulwark for its freedom. This was especially true when the world body proclaimed its devotion to broad principles of social and economic justice and developed specialized organizations to bring such aims to reality in every part of the war-torn earth.

When the United Nations took official action to put down the aggression in Korea in the summer of 1950 the Republic of Panama was quick to pledge its support to this great project in international coöperation. On August 3, 1950 the government authorized the use of the national merchant marine in support of the war purposes of the United Nations, the free transit of United Nations forces across the isthmus, the use of supplies and resources, including farm lands, and the reactivation of World War II bases and such others as might be necessary for training and defense.[47]

This last move was especially significant in view of Panama's refusal, after 1946, to consent to United States use of these properties on a bilateral basis, a controversy discussed in the next chapter herein. Now Dr. Carlos Brin, chief of the Panamanian delegation at Lake Success, declared that his country would offer the sites without any strings attached, and for *any* plan worked out by the United Nations command! It seems to this writer that no more striking evidence could be found of Panama's attitude toward the world organization as compared to any other agency upon earth. Nor is the picture altered by the likelihood that United States forces would in all probability be the United Nations groups sent to occupy the bases. That would not change the all-important fact, to a Panamanian, that the action was being taken by, and in the name of, the United Nations rather than by the power of the "*Gringo* Colossus."

In August of 1950 the Cabinet took an historic step: it authorized recruitment of an army of Panamanian volunteers to fight under the United Nations banner in Korea. This was the act of a nation which had never sent an armed force to fight beyond its borders, and which indeed had not had any army at all for more than forty-five years except for the small beach and security watches of World War II.[48] This circumstance affords another insight into Panamanian views toward the United States, and toward the United Nations. Dr. Brin had this to say on October 7, 1950:

We called for volunteers, and got 1,000 in a short time. But we were never able to find out from Washington what plans it had for such forces (referring to the fact that the over-all command of United Nations forces in Korea had been awarded to United States authorities) . . . so we stopped the enlistment procedure.[49]

Señor Brin went on to declare that forces could be raised from Central and South American nations, merged into a single United Nations unit, and be trained to use the facilities of the abandoned bases. Such a program would of course preclude any return to a status of exclusive United States occupation of the sites. The presence of a foreign armed force so close to the Canal Zone, regardless of what authority it might claim to serve, would doubtless be strenuously opposed by the military leadership of the United States.[50]

Panama holds membership in the following specialized agencies of the United Nations: the International Labor Organization, the International Monetary Fund, the International Civil Aviation Organization, the International Bank for Reconstruction and Development, the Postal Union, the International Telecommunication Union, and the Interim Commission of the International Trade Organization. The Republic signed the Constitution of the International Refugee Organization, thus committing itself to the program of aiding displaced persons, but had not at the time of this writing taken its place as a member of I.R.C. Panama is likewise not a member of UNESCO, or of the World Health Organization, or the Inter-Governmental Maritime Consultative Organization,[51] or of the World Meteorological Organization.[52]

The Republic has been active in the work of the United Nations Economic Commission for Latin America, upon which its representatives have been Pablo Abad, Miguel

Brandao, and Gilberto Orillac.[53] Until December 31, 1948, Panama was one of the powers serving an elective term on the Commission on Human Rights, where it was represented by Dr. Alfaro, M. Amado, and M. de J. Quijano.[54] The Republic also was a member of the Sub-Commission on Freedom of Information and the Press, its term of service there expiring on December 31, 1949. During the meetings of the Second Session of the General Assembly Panama's delegates were at various times Dr. Alfaro, Jorge E. Boyd, José A. Sosa, Juan Reyes, and Manuel Guardia.[55]

Through the years since 1945 the men who have represented the Isthmian nation in the world organization have compiled an excellent record of coöperation and constructive action which has made their country a leader among the smaller nations. The statesmanship of Ricardo J. Alfaro, particularly, has made a lasting impression upon his colleagues. Harley A. Notter, Advisor to the Assistant Secretary of State for United Nations Affairs, has expressed to this writer a personal reaction which is probably an accurate expression of what many of those who have labored close to the world organization would say: "As the United Nations records indicate, Panama, since the establishment of the United Nations, has attached great importance to the World Organization . . . Panama has played an active role. . . ."

This record of accomplishment within the greatest project of international coöperation which the mind of man has yet conceived is the result of undeviating allegiance to a policy which the Government of Panama announced away back in the very dark days of 1942: the "leal colaboración de nuestra República a las Naciones Unidas."[56] Would that powers far greater than Panama had been equally true to the ideals which they at that time proclaimed! How different might be the state of the world in this year of mid-century.

Footnotes

CHAPTER TEN

Panama and the United Nations

1. *New York Times,* January 3, 1942.
2. Ezéquiel Padilla, "The American System and the World Organization," *Foreign Affairs,* October 1945, pp. 99-107; *Pan American Bulletin,* "The Americas and the War," Vol. LXXIX, July 1945, p. 406; and P. H. Bidwell, "Good Neighbors in the War and After," *Foreign Affairs,* Vol. XXI, April 1943, pp. 524-34.
3. U.S. State Department, *United Nations Conference on Food and Agriculture, Hot Springs, Virginia, May 18—June 3, 1943,* Conference Series No. 52 (Washington, 1943).
4. República de Panamá, Ministro de Relaciones Exteriores, *Memoria 1943-1944* (Panamá, 1945), p. lvii.
5. U.S. State Department, *First Session of the Council of the United Nations Relief and Rehabilitation Administration, Selected Documents,* Atlantic City, November 10, 1943 (Washington, 1944).
6. Panamá, Ministro de Relaciones Exteriores, *Memoria 1943-1944, supra,* p. lix.
7. Panamá, *Memoria 1943-1944, supra,* p. lxii.
8. Ralph Hancock, *The Rainbow Republics, Central America* (New York, 1947), p. 57. Also, Howell Davies, ed., *The South American Handbook 1946* (London, 1946), p. 624.
9. U.S. State Department, *International Bank for Reconstruction and Development—Articles of Agreement between the U.S.A. and Other Powers, Bretton Woods, New Hampshire, July 1-22, 1944,* Treaties Series No. 1502 (Washington, 1946), p. 1.
10. Panamá, *Memoria 1943-1944, supra,* p. lxii.
11. U.S. State Department, *Proceedings of the International Civil Aviation Conference, Chicago, November 1—December 7, 1944* (Washington, 1948), I, 49.
12. A. P. Whitaker, ed., *Inter-American Affairs 1944, Annual Survey No. 4* (New York, 1945), pp. 71-72.

13. U.S. State Department, *Proceedings of Civil Aviation Conference, supra,* I, 86-87, 476.
14. *Ibid.,* II, 1270.
15. *Ibid.,* p. 1257.
16. *Ibid.,* I, 346.
17. Ezéquiel Padilla, "The American System and the World Organization," *Foreign Affairs,* October 1945, p. 99.
18. See Chapter Nine, pp. 125-26, *supra.*
19. United Nations, Department of Public Information, *Yearbook of the United Nations, 1946-1947* (New York, 1948), pp. 46, 49.
20. Laurence Duggan, *The Americas, the Search for Hemispheric Security, op. cit.,* pp. 117-20.
21. *Ibid.,* p. 118.
22. U.S. State Department, *Bulletin,* April 1, 1945, publishing text of speech delivered the previous day by Nelson Rockefeller, Coördinator of Inter-American Affairs.
23. There were 46 states present at the outset. The American nations made 20 of these (Canada not being reckoned as one of the inter-American bloc). Beside Argentina, 2 Soviet satellites, Bylorussia and The Ukraine, were admitted. It was thought by some that their admission was a result of a compromise with Russia to counterbalance the acceptance of Argentina. See A. P. Whitaker, ed., *Inter-American Affairs 1945, op. cit.,* pp. 19-20. In an interview with this writer in April, 1950, Harley A. Notter, Advisor to the Assistant Secretary of State for United Nations Affairs expressed a personal view that there was "some basis" for this belief, emphasizing carefully, however, that he was only making a personal observation.
24. U.S. State Department, *Consultation Among the American Republics with Respect to the Argentine Situation,* Inter-American Series No. 29 (Washington, 1946).
25. A. P. Whitaker, ed., *Inter-American Affairs 1945, supra,* pp. 20-23.
26. Ricardo J. Alfaro, "La Intervención Colectiva de las Repúblicas Américanas," *Revista de Derecho Internacional* (Havana, December 1945), pp. 153-62.
27. United Nations, Department of Public Information, *United Nations Chronology, 1942-1947* (Lake Success, 1947).
28. *Panama Star and Herald,* January 11, 1946.
29. *United Nations Yearbook, 1946-1947, supra,* pp. 308-12.
30. *Ibid.,* p. 572.
31. *Ibid.,* p. 210.
32. See Chapter Five, p. 64, *supra.*

33. Octavio Méndez Pereira has edited a published collection of Panamanian writings on this subject under the title, *Antologia del Canal, 1914-1939* (Panamá, 1939). Included are the following articles, in sequence: Eusebio A. Morales, "El Tratado del Canal y la República de Panamá—su historia e interpretación"; Ricardo J. Alfaro, "Nota oficial de la Secretaría de Relaciones Exteriores sobre el status de Panamá"; Samuel Lewis, "Nuestra Soberanía sobre el Canal"; D. Narciso Garay, "Conclusiones sobre el status de Panamá"; and Harmodio Arias, "Factores que contribuyen a darle el Canal de Panamá un status internacional."

34. Norman J. Padelford, *The Panama Canal in Peace and War, op. cit.*, pp. 183 *et seq.*, reviews development of the Canal Zone's status *vis-à-vis* the various branches of the U.S. government and cites judicial interpretations.

35. In January 1921, a U.S. District Court judge in the Canal Zone so ruled and stirred up a storm of protest by going even further to declare Panama "a protectorate" of the U.S. See *Diario Nacional*, Panamá, January 14-16, 1921.

36. United Nations, General Assembly, *Report of the Special Committee created to examine information on Non-Self Governing Territories under Article 73(e) of the Charter* (New York, October 1, 1948), a mimeographed release, pp. 2-4.

37. *Ibid.*, Appendix B (II), p. 39.

38. United Nations, Department of Public Information, *Yearbook of the United Nations, 1947-1948* (New York, 1949), p. 321.

39. *Ibid.*, p. 215.

40. Article in *American Bar Association Journal*, Vol. 35, No. 8, August 1949, pp. 688 *et seq.*—Louis B. Sohn, "The Development of International Law—Declaration on Rights and Duties of States."

41. *Ibid.*, p. 689.

42. *Report of the Section of International and Comparative Law of the American Bar Association*, printed in the Official Program of the 72nd Annual Meeting of the Association at St. Louis, September 5-9, 1949, pp. 150-51, portion entitled, "Codification of International Law."

43. United Nations, Department of Public Information, *Weekly Bulletin of the United Nations*, Vol. VIII, No. 10, for November 15, 1949, p. 613.

44. *Ibid.*

45. República de Panamá, *Memoria 1943-1944*, of Ministro de Relaciones Exteriores, *op. cit.*, p. xlvii, commenting on Dumbarton Oaks and plans for a world organization generally.

46. Quoting from Enrique A. Jiménez in a letter written to the

editor of the *Saturday Evening Post,* and published in that magazine November 13, 1948.

47. *Panama Star and Herald,* August 4, 1950. See also the *New York Times* for same date.

48. In the original disbanding of the Panamanian army the U.S. had taken a decisive role. *See* U.S. State Department, Dispatch, from Minister John Barrett, at Panama, to Hay, November 21, 1904.

49. *Chicago Daily News,* October 7, 1950; *Panama Star and Herald,* October 8, 1950.

50. *Ibid.;* also *Washington Evening Star,* Washington, D. C., October 7, 1950.

51. United Nations, Department of Public Information, *United Nations Maritime Conference, Geneva 1948. Final Act and Related Documents* (Lake Success, 1948).

52. *United Nations Yearbook, 1946-1947, supra,* p. 866. *United Nations Yearbook, 1947-1948, supra,* p. 970.

53. *United Nations Yearbook, 1947-1948,* p. 705.

54. *Ibid.,* p. 701.

55. *Ibid.,* p. 315.

56. Quoting Dr. Jesús Vázquez Gayoso, Director, Universidad del Aire, Universidad Nacional de Panamá, in the Frontispiece, *Una Nación en Guerra, op. cit.*

CHAPTER ELEVEN

Present Day Problems: Prospect

IT SEEMS FITTING to close this work with a consideration of recent problems which are of a continuing nature and likely to affect Panama's role in any project of international coöperation. The issues which today have the greatest bearing on Panama's part in the United Nations, in the Inter-American System, and upon her bilateral relations with other powers, notably the United States, are (1) the domestic political situation, (2) communism and the far-flung "Cold War" between East and West, and (3) the precarious nature of the national economy.

Panama's part in any project of international coöperation, or any other phase of foreign relations, is likely to be in the future, as it has always been in the past, conditioned fundamentally by domestic politics. The Panamanian people have characteristically been intensely conscious of their public affairs, and there is a greater degree of mass participation in such matters than is generally the case in Latin America. Partisan feelings have run especially high since the end of World War II, and several issues growing out of, or closely connected with, Panama's part in that conflict still stir up political furor and keep this always turbulent nation in a state of public confusion. Since 1940 no less than nine changes have occurred in the office of president of the Republic, and the second half of the century began with the most chaotic situation prevailing in the City of Panama which that ancient city had seen in a very long time, as a consequence of the Arias *coup d'état* late in 1949.

The Peoples Party is the Panamanian manifestation of the world Communist movement. The Workers Federation, the Workers General Union, and the Farmers Federation are other Red "front" organizations. They constitute a weak branch of communism by the standards of the powerful Red organizations in Cuba or Brazil, but the most menacing feature of it is its liaison with a Communist-dominated labor union in the Canal Zone. This is the United Public Workers, which was expelled from the C.I.O. on February 16, 1950 on the ground that it was a Communist-dominated organization.[1] An A.F. of L. source estimated in 1949 that the United Public Workers then controlled 5,000 of the 15,000 native workers employed within the Canal Zone.[2] On March 19, 1949, the Foreign Office in Panama City ordered the immediate expulsion of Max Brodsky, regional director of this union, on the ground of his Communist connections. Brodsky had long been denied admittance to the Canal Zone, but had directed his union's activities from Panamanian soil, where he had held a temporary residence permit since 1947 for "business purposes."[3]

A little over a year later, on April 29, 1950, the Republic declared all-out war on communism. A decree of that date, signed by President Arnulfo Arias and every member of his Cabinet, outlawed the Communist "Peoples Party" as

the absolute negation of all democracy, contrary to Christian civilization, and a menace to all democratic regimes. . . . All propaganda, activity, or agitation of a Communist character is contrary to the democratic regime of the Republic, . . . and

PRESENT DAY PROBLEMS: PROSPECT 169

has the sole objective of undermining the stability of democratic institutions.

The decree stated that the action was being taken because the Panama Canal constituted "a most important key in the defense of this continent, and this country is bound by virtue of bilateral treaties, to contribute to the protection and joint security of the United States of America." All Panamanian citizens, and aliens residing upon the Isthmus, were admonished to form a solid front against Communist infiltration.[4]

These actions in the Republic, and within the Canal Zone have shut off open Communist activity upon the Isthmus. But it is well demonstrated by past history that subversive movements often thrive underground, and it may be doubted that driving communism to cover in Panama will weaken or destroy it. For one thing many of the seeds upon which communism and its propaganda have fed are still germinating trouble and little has been done to kill these roots of discontent. Among points urged by those following the "party line" in Panama are (1) demands that the annual rentals paid to Panama for use of the Canal Zone be increased, (2) that idle lands in the Canal Zone be turned over to Panamanian farmers for cultivation, (3) that the Zone Commissaries be abolished, and that the Zone government relinquish its police powers such as the licensing of automobiles and drivers.

The great talking point of Communist agitation on the Isthmus is the racial question. Within the Republic of Panama there is, practically speaking, absolutely no "color line," and intermingling of the many races is an everyday fact. But across the border in the Canal Zone a policy of segregating "Gold" and "Silver" (i.e., Caucasian and others) employees has been effective in one form or another since construction days, when the two types of coin were used to pay off the two classes of workers.⁵ Despite recent desultory official motions to end it segregation is still practiced in virtually all public places. This policy is particularly hateful to Mestizos and other non-Africans who find themselves driven pell mell into "Silver" clubhouses, swimming pools, housing areas, and theaters with the dark-skinned, West Indian English-speaking Negroes and barred from "Gold" establishments, since any degree of color, however slight, seems to class one in *Yanqui* eyes as "Silver." A recent substitution of the terms "National" and "Local" for the old expressions "Gold" and "Silver" does not of course change the situation.

Communists in Panama have been quick to exploit the inconsistency between talk of "civil rights" at Washington, D. C., and performance at Canal Headquarters on Balboa Heights. Serious race riots have occurred at Balboa in the La Boca "Silver" quarters, and anti-*Yanqui* demonstrations have been staged in Panama. It is the mission of Isthmian Communists to contribute to the "Cold War" by causing as much embarrassment as possible to the North Americans in Panama. In view of the strategic importance of the Panama Canal in any hemispheric defense plan, the potential danger of this Red activity is easily understood.

On July 22, 1949, President Truman signed a bill to bring all employees of the Panama Canal under Civil Service.⁶ This Act will probably be construed to place them under the "Loyalty Oath" laws, and require of them "no-strike against the Government" affidavits, which have been required of regular U.S. Civil Service employees since World War II.⁷ It would seem, however, that real Communists would have no compunction about making such affidavits with their fingers crossed and remaining on the pay roll and within the strategic Canal Zone, for it is a well-known Communist tenet that any duplicity is justified if it contributes to fulfilling an assigned mission. Likely to be of much more practical value in ferreting out Communists and their sympathizers is an apparent decision of Canal Zone authorities to sign future contracts with a newly organized C.I.O. affiliate instead of the United Public Workers. The loss of the affiliation with the C.I.O. by the U.P.W. has probably weakened the effectiveness of the Communist front in Panama more than any governmental moves to outlaw it.

The *Nacionalista* and *Hispanidad* parties in Panama are of course ideologically opposed to communism. But in times past they have collaborated with Communists in demonstrations to harass the United States. The cult of *Hispanidad* in Panama bears a considerable relation to the *Sinarquists* of Mexico, and indeed the expression *Sinarquismo* is sometimes heard upon the isthmus. The movement is fundamentally anti-*Yanqui,* and even anti-Pan American. It has expressed an affinity for Franco Spain, and clings to the ideal of Hispanic culture and heritage.[8] It feeds upon the latent isthmian fears and suspicions of *El Coloso del Norte,*[9] covets a role for Panama of "whipping boy" for "*Gringo* Imperialism" and exploits to the fullest degree any sympathy it can arouse elsewhere in Latin America for Panama in her "bondage" to the *Yanqui* cultural impact and economic power.[10] All too often in other Latin American countries writers will cite Panama as an example of North American imperialism, which is still believed to be an insidious menace.[11] Panamanian nationalists hasten to seize upon this outside "authority" to bolster their cry that *no* deal can be made with the United States without surrendering *something.*

The controversy over the wartime defense bases gave

the *Nacionalistas* an opportunity to stir up a major crisis between Panama and the United States in 1946-48. As has been noted, the Panamanian government under President de la Guardia had made these base sites available to the United States during the Second World War.[12] The North American occupancy of these areas was to be for the duration and "for not more than one year after hostilities shall cease."[13] The United States continued to hold the bases more than one year after V-J Day, contending that the agreement would be legally effective until one year after the definitive treaty of peace. Panama insisted that a continued occupation after V-J Day, plus one year, constituted an infringement upon its sovereignty. Upon the rock of this controversy much of the stored up good feeling of the Roosevelt years was dashed to pieces.[14]

When the United States Ambassador, General Frank T. Hines, submitted the draft of a new treaty in December 1946, calling for a twenty-year extension of the U.S. leaseholds on thirteen sites,[15] the *Nacionalistas* considered this too good an opportunity to let pass for Panama once again to play before the eyes of her Latin American neighbors the time-honored role of prime victim of "*Yanqui* Imperialism." Although President Enrique Jiménez had put his signature to the treaty, the National Assembly had yet to ratify it and when they met to consider it a mob of 10,000 Nationalist hotheads marched on the legislature brandishing clubs, stones, guns, and machetes, and howling against *Gringo* Imperialism.[16] The terror-stricken Assembly turned down the treaty 51-0 in scenes very reminiscent of 1926 when another treaty with the United States had met a similar fate.[17]

The alleged "cavalier" methods of Ambassador Hines, if they were used as his critics said, undoubtedly played into the hands of those who instigated this uprising. He was accused of bringing the brusque, authoritarian manner of the military into a situation where great diplomatic finesse was required. Such a system of blustering, veiled threats, patronizing attitudes, and seeming impatience with traditional Latin delays and arguments would all have been characteristics which Panamanians had come to find most distasteful in *Gringos*. His appointment to the post so ably filled during the war years by the experienced career diplomat, Edwin C. Wilson, was probably a mistake in any case. There is quite enough of the U.S. Military on the isthmus at Balboa Heights without turning over to them the Embassy in Bella Vista as well. Washington seemed to take this forceful lesson to heart, for Hines was soon replaced by a veteran Latin American expert from the State Department—Monnett B. Davis. The question of the bases, however, was destined to remain unsolved up to the time of this writing.[18]

Ambassador Davis was eminently successful in effecting cordial relationships with Minister of Foreign Affairs Ernesto Jaen de la Guardia, and with his successor, Ignacio Molino, Jr. under the new President, Domingo Díaz Arosemena. Tangible evidence of this was the signing on March 31, 1949, of a civil aviation agreement which provided for the development of the $8,000,000 Tocumen Airport.[19] The Nationalists immediately raised the familiar cry that the United States was using still another insidious device to control Panama, and they repeated their 1946 tactics of storming the Assembly. This time, however, the government of Domingo Díaz Arosemena acted with courage and firmness and broke up the rioting with tear gas, gunfire, and mounted police charges. Behind this protection the Assembly ratified the treaty by 27 votes to 12.[20]

The *Nacionalista-Hispanidad* movement continued to

grow, however. The retrenchment in U.S. military and civil service establishments in the Canal Zone accompanying post-war demobilization had a pronounced effect in reducing Panama's volume of business. Following the killing of the Hines-Jiménez Treaty the North American forces had been swiftly withdrawn from the thirteen wartime bases in the Republic's territory, and this had produced an additional jolt to the national economy for personnel at the bases in the Republic had spent their earnings liberally in the shops and *cantinas* nearby, and in addition many Panamanian laborers employed at the bases were thrown out of work. To increase the general uncertainty of the economic future many isthmians learned with foreboding that Dictator Somoza of Nicaragua was holding out all sorts of blandishments to persuade the United States to build a new inter-oceanic canal there.[21] It was easy to imagine that the northern republic might very well decide to do just that in view of strained relations with Panama, and the result would be a diversion of hundreds of millions of dollars from the isthmus and the relegation of the Panama Canal to a position quite subordinate to that of the new waterway.

It might be supposed that the Nationalists as the assassins of the Hines-Jiménez Treaty would have received the blame for this lag in the nation's economic outlook. But it seems to be the practice in most lands to blame the party in power for the effects of hard times. The rank and file of Panama's working class turned to the *Nacionalistas,* spearheaded by Arnulfo Arias and his Authentic Revolutionary Party as the principal opposition and practical alternative to the fumbling government which they felt was doing nothing to alleviate their hardships. The Revolution of November 1949 which violently overthrew President Daniel Chanis[22] (who had succeeded from the vice presidency upon the death of Diaz in the previous summer) was, on the whole, welcomed by the masses. Furthermore, it had been long expected even by those who were holding on so desperately to the reins of power. The venerable Díaz Arosemena expressed the thought to this writer not long before his death that "constitutional government" was functioning atop a volcano.

Arnulfo Arias, who emerged triumphant from the imbroglio of November and December, 1949, had long been the darling of the laboring masses, in addition to *Hispanidad* and Nationalist elements. He had made an exciting run for the Presidency against Díaz Arosemena in 1948. The result hung in the balance for three months before the National Election Jury announced on August 7, 1948, that Díaz was victor by 2,400 votes. Since Díaz was the candidate of the pro-government forces, and Panama's national elections usually follow a typical Latin American pattern, it is not hard to imagine that the narrow official margin of victory may very well have been a manufactured triumph. In any case the Arias forces never conceded it, and after the *coup d'état* of the year's end in 1949 the National Election Jury reversed itself and declared that Arias had won in 1948 after all! This action gave a color of legality to the Arias presidency. This writer is fairly well convinced that it represented as well a belated acknowledgment of the factual outcome of the 1948 canvass.

In 1949 and 1950 President Arias had obvious strong support among the masses. No visitor to Panama at the time could fail to note the fact. However, he retained the bitter hostility of powerful enemies and domestic isthmian politics remained very unsettled through the winter of 1950-1951. In May 1951 a typical Panamanian revolution occurred when Arias gave the opponents of his régime both excuse and opportunity to rise against him by attempting to suspend the Constitution of 1946. After three days of bloody rioting he was overthrown and imprisoned. His loyal supporters defended him to the last behind barricades in the *presidencia*. The scales were tipped against him when the national police obeyed the orders of the Assembly which had decreed his deposition. The Vice-President, Alcibíades Arosemena, was sworn in as President of the Republic on May 9, 1951.

The national police, whose intervention was decisive in the May uprising in 1951, always constitute the imponderable equation in Panamanian politics. They are the only organized armed force in the nation. Their leader, Colonel José Antonio Remón, is a shrewd, silent man who prefers to exercise his enormous influence behind the scene. No regime of the past ten years has been able to hold power without his support, and he has not hesitated to shift his support as he has sensed changing tides of popular opinion.

The revolution in the spring of 1951 proved once again the basic instability of the executive power in Panama. No nation has been more attracted to the Latin American concept of the "Divine Right of Revolution." The stress and strain of conflicting personalities and the divisive force of factionalism must always be taken into consideration in attempting to appraise the isthmian republic. There is no reason to suppose that the future will not be completely normal in this respect. Political instability is essentially a domestic concern, however. Successive goverments have made relatively few radical changes in foreign policy the past few years. That is why Panama's sister republics have usually taken a calm view of the rise and fall of factions, parties, and men.

The shaky nature of Panama's economy and failure to solve problems arising from it were major factors in discrediting both Arnulfo Arias and the preceding Díaz-

PRESENT DAY PROBLEMS: PROSPECT 177

Chanis regime. One of the worst crises of an economic character was a developing threat to the Isthmian Republic's position among the principal maritime states of the world. As has been noted elsewhere in this work,[23] World War II had increased the tonnage of shipping registered under Panama's flag tenfold. Even in the post-war years the merchant marine of the Isthmian Republic continued to grow, because it had been discovered that operating costs, including tax charges, were lower under the flag of Panama. Joel Medina, Director of the *Sección Consular y de Naves*, established cordial relations between his government and many big shipping concerns and did much to foster the growth of the Republic's merchant marine.

These developments had irked merchant seamen, for wages, working conditions, and safety precautions were under Panamanian law at a level considerably below the standards required under the shipping laws of the United States. The International Transport Workers Federation soon took up the grievances of the merchant sailors. After desultory efforts to force shipowners to grant them concessions, without avail, they took their case to the convention of the International Federation at Rotterdam in August 1949. There they found sympathy, and leaders at the convention began talking about a world-wide boycott of registered Panamanian shipping.[24] The government of President Chanis then awoke to a realization of the threat which this situation carried for Panama's economy and its importance as a world maritime power.

The Republic began to publish data claiming that its labor code matched any in the world, and that its wages ranked third in the international scale, behind only the United States and Canada. It pointed to its long record of support of the International Labor Organization, now a specialized agency of the United Nations. It pointed not only to its new Labor Code of 1948 but to other legislation aimed to improve working conditions on board ship. It insisted that the great majority of Panamanian ships were modern and in full compliance with the International Convention of Safety of Life at Sea and of the Loadline Convention.[25] The ITWF professed not to be impressed by any of this and the proposed boycott was put on the agenda of the Rotterdam Conference.

At this juncture the Panama government named two special emissaries to go to Rotterdam to try to stave off the threatened sanctions. These men were Carlos Berguido, Jr., Special Advisor and Coördinator of Shipping for the Republic's Washington Embassy, and Bernardino Gonzales Ruiz, Panamanian Minister to Great Britain.[26] Berguido conducted the negotiations alone because Ruiz was unavoidably detained from getting to Rotterdam in time for the meeting.

Señor Berguido was an excellent choice for this mission. He had long been recognized as an authority in Latin American Admiralty Law, and had written manuals for masters and seamen, and instructions for ships at sea and in foreign ports.[27] At Rotterdam he persuaded the International Federation to defer boycott action until after a Conference at Geneva on December 5, 1949, at which the Panamanian government guaranteed to have present qualified representatives of the shipping interests. In the meantime it was agreed that the charges should be submitted to a committee of Inquiry of the International Labor Organization, which is now an agency of the United Nations.

Before the Geneva meeting could be held the Revolution had occurred in Panama which brought Arias to power. This upheaval furnished a very legitimate excuse for postponing the conference, and the prolonged investi-

cast a shadow over international coöperation. But this feeling is obviously receding and does not appear to pose any threat to Panama's loyal support of either the Organization of American States or of the United Nations. The present climate of opinion upon the Isthmus, both in the government and out, is most favorable to the ideal of international coöperation. Panamanians regard the United Nations as still the best great hope of mankind and this fact in itself furnishes a most satisfactory observation with which to bring this study to a close.

Footnotes

CHAPTER ELEVEN

Present Day Problems: Prospect

1. *New York Times,* February 17, 1950.
2. Victor Reisel, "The Labor Front," in the *Philadelphia Inquirer,* February 10, 1949.
3. *Philadelphia Inquirer,* March 20, 1949.
4. *Panama Sunday Star and Herald,* April 30, 1950.
5. Paul Blanshard, *Democracy and Empire in the Caribbean* (New York, 1947), Chap. III of Part III, entitled, "Race and Democracy at the Panama Canal," pp. 238-43.
6. *Philadelphia Evening Bulletin,* July 22, 1949.
7. Public Law 491, Section 202, Title II (General Provisions), p. 19, is an example of the "loyalty oath" statutes which have been made applicable to the Canal Zone.
8. M. de J. Quijano, "Una Campaña Antifascista" (Tomo I en *La Ruta Liberal y Democrática;* Panamá, 1943), pp. 5, 42, 111, and 153. See also Stephen Duggan, *The Two Americas, An Interpretation,* chapter entitled, "Hispanidad," p. 231.
9. Article in *Newsweek,* "Panama: Better Feeling," April 25, 1949. See also comment in Sidney Shalett, "Can We Defend the Panama Canal?," *op. cit.*
10. Scott Seegers, "The World's Best Business Set-Up," art. in *Inter-American,* for August 1946. See also "Panama: No Empare-

dados," unsigned art. in *Time*, April 18, 1949. See also Luis Marden, "Panama, Bridge of the World," *op. cit.*, and Ralph Hancock, *The Rainbow Republics—Central America*, *op. cit.*, pp. 40-46, 93-98, 180.

11. For example: Leopoldo Zea, *Dos Etapas del Pensamiento en Hispanoamérica* (Mexico, 1949), p. 131, quotes Francisco Bilbao [*Obras Completas*, Buenos Aires, 1866] . . . "los Estados Unidos le preocupa por su vecindad con la América hispana. Sabe que tratarán de extender su influencia dominando a la débil Hispanoamérica, Los Estados Unidos . . . extienden cada día mas sus garras en esa partida de caza que han emprendido contra . . . ayer Texas, después, el norte de Mexico . . . Panamá."

12. See Chapter Eight, pp. 117-18, *supra*.

13. Austin F. MacDonald, *Latin American Politics and Government* (New York, 1949). p. 617.

14. Sidney Shalett, "Can We Defend the Panama Canal?," *supra*. See also Morton C. Steinberg, "Sea Level Canal, a Vital Defense Need," art. in *Everybody's Weekly* (magazine section of the *Philadelphia Sunday Inquirer*), December 26, 1948.

15. Victor F. Goytía, *La Función Geografica del Istmo* (Panamá, 1948, pp. 219-20. This book contains a discussion of a Panamanian's reaction to this controversy in the chapter entitled, "Una Nueva Experiencia," pp. 208-23.

16. Sidney Shalett, *supra*.

17. See Chapter Five, pp. 62-65, *supra*.

18. Michael J. Mansfield, *The Panama Bases; Report of an inquiry into the circumstances and the effects of the rejection by the National Assembly of Panama of an agreement to extend U.S. occupancy of installations required for defense of the Canal Zone* (Washington: Government Printing Office, 1948), 13 pp.

19. U.S. State Department, *Air Transport Services Agreement between the U.S.A. and Panama*, Treaties Series No. 1932 (Harry S. Truman, 1945-   ), (Washington, 1949).

20. *New York Times*, April 9, 1949; *Newsweek*, April 25, 1949.

21. Austin F. MacDonald, *supra*, p. 617. See also "Plans of the Atomic Age for the Big Ditch," unsigned article in the *Philadelphia Inquirer*, November 10, 1946.

22. The developing revolution can be traced through the following articles: *Newsweek*, May 2, 1949, p. 40; *Time*, June 13, 1949, p. 35; *Time*, November 28, 1949, p. 28; *Newsweek*, December 5, 1949, pp. 38-39; *Time*, December 5, 1949, p. 38. Also *New York Times*, November 20-25, 1949.

23. See Chapter Eight, pp. 107-108, *supra*.

24. "Panama Deflects Shipping Boycott," art. in the *New York Times*, August 31, 1949.

25. These points are well summarized in an article by Carlos Berguido, Jr., "The Rights of a Seaman on a Ship under Panamanian Registry," Temple University *Law Quarterly*, Vol. XIX, No. 4, April 1946 (Philadelphia, Pennsylvania).

26. "Panama Will Try to Avert Boycott," *New York Times*, September 2, 1949. See also John Bunker, "Tiny Panama Gets Sea Legs," art. in *Christian Science Monitor*, February 6, 1950. Also Laurence M. Breece, "R. P. Merchant Marine is a Real Asset," reprinted address in *Panama Star and Herald* (English ed.), March 2, 1950.

27. Carlos Berguido, Jr., and Jorge Fabrega P., *Manual for Masters and Seamen on Ships under the Panamanian Flag, op. cit.*

28. *New York Times*, April 19, 1950.

29. Arnold Beichman, "Red 'Phantom Fleet' Sails Under Panama Flag: Boycott War Looms," art. in *The New Leader*, for April 15, 1950.

30. *New York Times*, April 19, 1950.

31. República de Panamá, Ministerio de Hacienda y Tesoro sección consular y de naves, *Lista de las Naves Incritas definitivamente en el Registro de la Marina Mercante Nacional* (Panamá 31 de Mayo, 1949), lists nearly 750 ships under R. P. registry. The number is still growing.

32. Editorial, *New York Times*, November 24, 1949.

33. See Chapter Eight, pp. 109-10, *supra*.

34. See Chapter Eight, p. 110, *supra*.

35. Radio Newscast, Columbia Broadcasting System, December 14, 1949. See also "U.S.-Panama Status Called Normal Now," *New York Times*, March 28, 1950, quoting E. G. Miller, U.S. Assistant Secretary of State, for Latin American Affairs.

36. *New York Times* for January 26, 1950.

37. "Panama—Three Presidents," art. in *Newsweek*, December 5, 1949, p. 39, says: ". . . the reception given him (Arias) last week indicated he had not lost the support of Panama's man in the street, the workers, and some of the students to whom his flamboyant nationalism appeals."

BIBLIOGRAPHY

List of References Consulted

I. BIBLIOGRAPHICAL AIDS

For the background of this study several general bibliographical aids were employed. Inasmuch as the official publications of the Government of Panama were to be an important source of material the *Guide to the Official Publications of the Other American Republics:—Panama,* compiled by John de Noia for the Library of Congress (Washington, 1947), was quite useful. The select list of publications contained in the annual supplements of Lewis Hanke, ed., *The Handbook of Latin American Studies, 1936-* (Harvard University Press), was often consulted, as was Ronald Hilton, ed., *Hispanic Source Materials in the United States* (Toronto, 1942). Liberal use was also made of bibliographic material listed in the five volumes of A. P. Whitaker, ed., *Inter-American Affairs, An Annual Survey* (New York, 1942-46), in the *Hispanic American Historical Review,* a quarterly published by the Duke University Press, and in R. A. Humphreys, *Latin America, A Selective Guide to Publications in English* (London, 1949). The work which the author was able to do upon the Isthmus of Panama was to some extent facilitated by Roscoe R. Hill's *The National Archives of Latin America* (Harvard University Press, 1945), and by the earlier publication of J. B. Childs, *The Memorias of the Republics of Central America and of the Antilles* (Washington, 1932). In the field of periodicals and newspapers, mention should be made of the *New York Times Index,* of the *National Geographic Magazine Cumulative Index, 1899-1949* (Washington, 1950), and of C. Shelby, *Latin American Periodicals currently received in the Library of Congress and in the Library of the Department of Agriculture* (Washington, 1945). Some use was also made of the old reference of the Pan American Union, *Bibliography on Relations between the United States and Panama* (Washington, 1924).

II. MANUSCRIPT SOURCES

A. THE NATIONAL ARCHIVES, Washington, D. C.

Very extensive use was made of Dispatches, Notes, and Instruc-

BIBLIOGRAPHY 187

tions to Ministers and Consuls of the United States, in Panama, and of Notes and Dispatches from U.S. Ministers and Consuls, in Panama, to the State Department. These are catalogued in the National Archives, Foreign Affairs Section, in five groups.

1. Notes from the Department to the Panamanian Legation, 1903-6.
2. Notes from the Panamanian Legation to the Department, 1903-6.
3. Dispatches from Panama, 1903-6 (Ministerial and Consular)
4. Dispatches from Panama (Ministerial and Consular) and Instructions to the Legation at Panama, 1906-10.
5. Dispatches from Panama (Ministerial and Consular) and Instructions to the Legation at Panama, 1910-29.

The foregoing divisions of documents are filed in three systems in the Foreign Affairs Section. The first three groups, covering the years 1903-6, are bound in large volumes, and indexed in the Numerical Files of State Department messages. The documents of the years 1906-10 are mixed, some being bound, some being held in box files. All are indexed as part of the Numerical Filing System. The documents of the years 1910-29 are also mixed, being partially held in bound volumes and partially in box files. They are all indexed as part of Decimal Filing System of the State Department. Papers for the years 1906-29 are mingled with State Department matter affecting many nations besides Panama, although occasionally an entire volume or file may be devoted to Panama.

In any case, the criterion for scholarly search in these papers is *the date* of the document in question. All are indexed chronologically in the files of the Foreign Affairs Section, National Archives. In this study, the numerical or decimal file is sometimes added to the citation, where it designates a file containing related matter in which searchers in this field might find interest. But it is emphasized that the key to these papers is the *date* of the dispatch, note, or report in question.

Inasmuch as all of these documents for the years since 1924 are classified, citations after that year are by permission of the Department of State, Division of Historical Policy and Research.

B. THE LIBRARY OF CONGRESS, Division of Manuscripts, Library of Congress Annex, Washington, D. C.

1. The Papers and Correspondence of Theodore Roosevelt. Arranged chronologically, incoming, and outgoing.
2. The Papers of Elihu Root. Arranged according to personal and official categories, incoming, and outgoing.
3. The Papers of John Barrett, U.S. Minister to Panama.

C. OFFICE OF NAVAL RECORDS AND LIBRARY, Navy Department, Washington, D. C.

1. The Administrative History of the Atlantic Fleet—typewritten and bound, 11 vols.

2. Office of the Commander in Chief, United States Fleet, Reports of Armed Guard officers.

3. War Diaries, Panama Sea Frontier, and 15th Naval District.

Note: The foregoing are, at present, classified state papers and may be examined only by qualified personnel.

D. THE ARCHIVO NACIONAL, Panama, Republic of Panama.

The writer made use of a few Panamanian state papers held in the Archivo Nacional. These were located in the Administrative Section of the Archivo, mostly in the Division of Government, and a few in the Division of War. The individual citations of these documents are contained in appropriate footnotes. Unfortunately conditions at the Archivo Nacional are such at the present time as to preclude orderly research. In 1933, because of governmental space requirements transfers of state papers to the Archivo was stopped and has not been resumed. But even before 1933 most documents of a "Classified" nature were not placed in the Archivo, but were held in the ministerial files. Access to them could only be obtained over the signature of the minister. Papers in Foreign Relations in the Archivo were never catalogued beyond the year 1906. However, the packets of papers have received careless handling over the years and now frequently do not correspond with the Index. The fact is that most information obtained for this work at the Archivo was found by chance, although attachés of the Section made every effort to be helpful. Juan Antonio Susto, a distinguished historian and geographical scholar, is working to correct these deficiencies but is hampered by lack of support from higher authorities.

E. CONSULATE GENERAL, Republic of Panama, Philadelphia, Pa.

1. Report of the Special Commission of Inquiry of the United Nations, International Labor Organization, into the charges of the International Transport Workers Federation regarding conditions aboard maritime vessels flying the flag of Panama. Mimeographed.

2. Interview, Fall 1942 (no spec. date), between Carlos Berguido, Jr., Consul General, and George Salvesen, Master, of the Panamanian merchant vessel *Troubadour*.

F. U.S. DEPARTMENT OF STATE, Division of Historical Policy and Research.

By special permission the author was allowed to examine the files of the Ministerial and Consular Reports, Dispatches, and Instructions to and from Panama for the period 1929-33, which are held in this office. All of these papers are contained in steel filing cabinets and are still classified documents. A card file, arranged chronologically under incoming and outgoing classifications, is the sole key for research. Documents are brought from the files by attendants and examined under supervision. All citations from these papers are by special permission of the Department of State, Historical Advisor.

III. OFFICIAL PRINTED SOURCES: UNITED STATES OF AMERICA

A. DEPARTMENT OF STATE.
Papers Relating to the Foreign Relations of the United States (Washington, 1902-21; and 1922-43)
Reports of U.S. Delegations to Conferences, etc.
To the Third International Conference of American States, Rio de Janeiro 1906 (Washington, 1907)
To the Fifth International Conference of American States, Santiago 1923 (Washington, 1923)
To the Sixth International Conference of American States, Havana 1928 (Washington, 1929)
To the Seventh International Conference of American States, Montevideo 1933 (Washington, 1934)
To the Inter-American Conference for the Maintenance of Peace, Buenos Aires 1936 (Washington, 1937)
To the Eighth International Conference of America States, Lima 1938 (Washington, 1941)
To the Meeting of the Foreign Ministers of the American Republics, Panama 1939 (Washington, 1940)
To the Second Meeting of the Foreign Ministers of the American Republics, Havana 1940 (Washington, 1941)
To the Third Meeting of the Ministers of Foreign Affairs of the American Republics, Rio de Janeiro 1942 (Washington, 1942)
To the Inter-American Conference on Problems of War and Peace, Mexico City 1945 (Washington, 1946)
To the Inter-American Conference for the Maintenance of Continental Peace and Security, Quitandinha, Brazil 1947 (Washington, 1948)
To the Ninth International Conference of American States, Bogotá 1948 (Washington, 1948)
Reports on United Nations Matters
United Nations Conference on Food and Agriculture, Hot Springs, Virginia 1943 (Washington, 1943)
United Nations Relief and Rehabilitation Administration, First Session of the Council, Atlantic City 1943 (Washington, 1944)

International Civil Aviation Conference, Chicago 1944 (Washington, 1948)
International Bank for Reconstruction and Development. . . . Articles of Agreement . . . at United Nations Monetary and Financial Conference, Bretton Woods, 1944 (Washington, 1946)
United Nations Conference on International Organization: Report to the President on the Results of the San Francisco Conference by the Secretary of State (Washington, 1945)
Treaties and Other International Acts Series, and Executive Agreements Series
Hull-Alfaro Treaty, Treaty Series No. 945 (F. D. Roosevelt), (Washington, 1939)
Lease of Defense Base Sites from Panama, Executive Agreements Series No. 359 (F. D. Roosevelt), (Washington, 1944)
Military Officers of U.S. detailed to Panama, Executive Agreements Series No. 414 (F. D. Roosevelt), (Washington, 1944)
Pan American Highway, Chorrera-Rio Hato, Executive Agreements Series No. 449 (F. D. Roosevelt), (Washington, 1945)
Trans-Isthmian Highway agr., U.S.-Panama, Executive Agreements Series No. 448 (F. D. Roosevelt), (Washington, 1945)
Air Transport Services Agreement, U.S.-Panama, Treaties Series No. 1932 (H. S. Truman), (Washington, 1949)
Miscellaneous State Department Publications
Bulletins: Individually cited in appropriate footnotes.
Memorandum of J. R. Clark on the Monroe Doctrine (Washington, 1930)
Press Releases: Individually cited in appropriate footnotes.
Program of the Interdepartmental Committee on Scientific and Cultural Cooperation (Washington, 1947)
Regulations to Govern Air Navigation in the Panama Canal Zone (Washington, 1934)
Report of Consultation Among the American Republics with Respect to the Argentine Situation (Washington, 1946)

Certain State Department publications carrying author's names are cited in this bibliography under their author. (Ex:—Kelchner, Warren, *Inter-American Conferences, 1826-1933* (Washington, 1933))

B. WAR DEPARTMENT

Annual Reports of the Governor of the Canal Zone—Fiscal 1917 (Washington, 1917); Fiscal 1918 (Washington, 1918); Fiscal 1919 (Washington, 1919)

C. NAVY DEPARTMENT

Bureau of Yards and Docks, *Building the Navy Bases in World War II* (Washington, 1947), 2 vols.

Official Communiqués of the Second World War (Washington, 1945), 3 vols.

D. THE COÖRDINATOR OF INTER-AMERICAN AFFAIRS

Americas United. A summary of the coöperative effort of the American Republics since September 1939 (Washington, 1943)

Basic Data on the Other American Republics (Washington, 1944)

E. THE CONGRESS OF THE UNITED STATES

The Congressional Record

House and Senate Documents

Individually cited in appropriate footnotes.

IV. OFFICIAL PRINTED SOURCES: REPUBLIC OF PANAMA

A. *Asamblea Nacional*

Leyes de Panamá, 1903-1945. Published in Panama, usually on a biennial basis. Volumes thus are for "1914-15," etc. Individual citations from this course may be found under appropriate footnotes. In recent years the set has been edited by Juan Antonio Susto, the Director of the Archivo Nacional, and later citations are therefore listed under his name.

Leyes aprobatorias de las convenciones suscritas en la sexta Conferencia panamericana celebrada en la Habana y de tratados, y convenciones entre la república de Panamá y otras naciones. Edición oficial especial autorized por la Asamblea Nacional (Panamá, 1929)

Leyes expedidas por la Asamblea nacional de Panamá en las sesiones ordinarias y extraordinarias de 1926 a 1927. Edición oficial revisada por el secretario de la Asamblea nacional, con vista de los respectivos originales de esa corporación (Panamá, 1927)

B. *Ministerio de Educación*

Programa de estudios superiores de los Institutos de legislación comparada y derecho internacional, investigaciónes sociales y económicas, investigaciónes folkloricas (Panamá, 1944)

C. *Ministerio de Hacienda y Tesoro*

Lista de las Naves Incritas definitivamente en el Registro de la Marina Mercante Nacional (Panamá, 1949)

D. *Secretaría de la Relaciones Exteriores* (after 1941 called *Ministerio de Relaciones Exteriores*)

Memoria, que el Ministro de la Relaciones Exteriores presenta a la Asamblea Nacional en sus sesiones ordinarias de 19- , etc. (Panamá, 1903-45)

These *Memorias* have sometimes been published on an annual and sometimes on a biennial basis. The following have been consulted for this study: 1906, 1908, 1910, 1912, 1913-14, 1916,

1918-20, 1922, 1924, 1926, 1928, 1930, 1932, 1934, 1936, 1936-38, 1938, 1938-40, 1940-42, 1943-44.

Controversia de límites entre Panamá y Costa Rica; respuesta de Panamá a los Estados Unidos (Panamá, 1921), 2 vol.

Discurso pronunciado por el presidente de la República de Panamá, doctor Juan Demostenes Arosemena, en la sesión inaugural de la reunión consultiva de los ministros de relaciones exteriores de las repúblicas Américanas (Panamá, 1939)

Documentos importantes relacionades con las negociaciones del tratado de 28 de julio de 1926 tomados de la Memoria de relaciones exteriores presentada a la Asamblea Nacional (Panamá, 1927)

Manifesto que dirige a la nación el excmo., señor presidente de la República don Ricardo Adolfo de la Guardia, con motivo de su segundo año de administración. Palabras dichas en la noche del 8 de Octubre de 1943, por las radio-difusoras nacionales (Panamá, 1943)

Méndez Pereira, Octavio, ed., *Acción Democrática Internacional, Tres Fechas, Secretaría de propaganda* (Panamá, 1943)

Ministro de Relaciones Exteriores, Departamento de Información publicación, *Constitución de la República* (Panamá, 1944)

E. *Gaceta Oficial* (Panamá, 1903-49.) Published for the most part on a daily basis. Individual references used herein are cited in the appropriate footnotes.

V. Publications of the League of Nations

Official Journal, Records of the Assembly 1920-37 (Geneva, 1920-37). Individual references in footnotes.

First Committee of the Assembly, *Relations between the League of Nations and the Pan American Union* (Geneva, 1935)

Final Report of the Board of Liquidation of the Assets of the League of Nations (Geneva, 1947)

L'Oeuvre de la Societé des Nations dans ses rapports avec le programme de la Septiéme Conférence Internacionale Américaine (Geneva, 1933)

Verbatim Reports of the Special Meeting of the Assembly at Geneva, March 1926 (Geneva, 1927)

VI. Publications of the United Nations

Handbook of the United Nations and Specialized Agencies (Lake Success, 1949)

Report of the Special Committee created to examine information on

Non-Self Governing territories under Article 73(e) of the Charter (New York, 1948)
Report of the Special Commission of the International Labor Organization to inquire into charges of the International Transport Workers Federation regarding conditions aboard maritime vessels flying the flag of Panama (Lake Success, 1950), (a document which the author was enabled to read by special courtesy of Señor Carlos Berguido. Not available to public perusal as of this writing)
United Nations Chronology, 1942-1947 (Lake Success, 1947)
United Nations Maritime Conference, Geneva 1948. Final Act and Related Documents (Lake Success, 1948)
Weekly Bulletin of the United Nations, and its Spanish version, *Boletín Semanal, Naciones Unidas* (Lake Success, 1946-50) Individual references cited in footnotes.
Yearbook of the United Nations, 1945-1946 (New York, 1947)
Yearbook of the United Nations, 1947-1948 (Lake Success, 1948)
Handbook of the United Nations and Specialized Agencies (Lake Success, 1949)

VII. Publications of Other Foreign Governments

A. Costa Rica
Documentos relativos al conflicto de jurisdicción territorial con la República de Panamá (San José, 1921)

B. Peru
Ideario y acción panaméricanistas del Presidente Prado. Estados Unidos, Cuba, Panamá, Venezuela, Colombia (Lima, 1944)

VIII. Publications of the Pan American Union

Acta final de la Reunión de consulta entre los Ministros de Relaciones Exteriores de las Repúblicas Américanas en Panamá (Panamá, 1939)
Actas de las sesiones de las sub-comisiones de "Mantenimiento de la Paz" y de "Cooperación Económica" (Panamá, 1939)
Actas des sesiones plenarias publicas (Panamá, 1939)
Bulletin of the Pan American Union (Washington) cited in individual footnotes.
Conferencia de Ministros y Directores de Educación de las Repúblicas Américanas. Primera (Panamá, 1943)
Inter-American Conferences, 1826-1948, Congress and Conferences Series No. 56 (Washington, 1949)
Inter-American Juridical Committee, *Preliminary Recommendation on Post War Programs* (Washington, 1942)

Inter-American Financial and Economic Advisory Committee, *Resume of Organization and Activities* (Washington, 1942)

Project of Organic Pact of the Inter-American System submitted to Ninth International Conference of American States (Washington, 1948)

Report on the Second Meeting of the Foreign Ministers of the American Republics, Havana 1940 (Washington, 1940)

Report of the Third Meeting of the Ministers of Foreign Affairs of the American Republics, Rio de Janeiro 1942 (Washington, 1942)

The writer has used much material published by the Pan American Union which is listed in this bibliography under the name of the author or editor. (Ex:—Charles G. Fenwick, "The Pact of Bogotá and other Juridical Decisions of the Ninth Conference," *Bulletin of the Pan American Union*, Vol. 82, August 1948)

IX. Publications of the Carnegie Endowment for International Peace

These are listed individually elsewhere in this bibliography under the names of their author or editor. (E:—James B. Scott, *International Conferences of American States, 1889-1928* (New York, 1931))

X. Printed Secondary Works
Listed by Author or Editor

Abbott, Willis J. *The Panama Canal.* (New York, 1922.)

Aguilera, Rodolfo. *Documentos historicos relativos a la fundación de la República de Panamá.* (Panamá, 1904.)

Alfaro, Ricardo J. *Commentary on Pan American Problems.* (Cambridge, Mass., 1938.)

———. *Costa Rica y Panamá en defensa de los quieron Paz y Amistad.* (Panamá, 1927.)

———. *Exposición de motivos del codigo civil y judicial de la República de Panamá.* (Panamá, 1917.)

———. *Los Acuerdos entre Panamá y los Estados Unidos.* (Panamá, 1943.)

———. *Panorama Internacional de America.* (Cambridge, 1938.)

Anesi, Carlos P. *La Carretera Panaméricana, "El Gran Premio de las Américas."* (Buenos Aires, 1938.)

Arias, Harmodio. *The Panama Canal, A Study in International Law.* (London, 1911.)

Arosemena, Justo. *Estudio sobre la idea de una liga américana.* (Lima, 1864.)

——. *Estudios constituciónales sobre los gobiernos de América latina.* (Paris, 1878), 2 vols.
——. *Proyecto de tratado para formar una liga suraméricana.* (Lima, 1865.)
Backus, Richard C. and Eder, Phanor J. *A Guide to the Law and Legal Literature of Colombia.* (Washington, 1943.)
Bailey, Thomas A. *The Policy of the United States toward the Neutrals 1917-1918.* (Baltimore, 1942.)
Ball, M. Margaret. *The Problem of Inter-American Organization.* (Palo Alto, Calif., 1944.)
Bannon, John F., and Dunne, Peter M. *Latin America, An Historical Survey.* (Milwaukee, 1947.)
Beals, Carleton. *The Coming Struggle for Latin America.* (Philadelphia, 1938.)
Bemis, Samuel F. *The Latin American Policy of the United States.* (New York, 1943.)
Berguido, Carlos, Jr., and Fabrega P., Jorge. *A Manual for Masters and Seamen on Ships under the Panamanian Flag.* (Philadelphia, 1949.)
Bishop, Farnham. *Panama, Past and President.* (New York, 1916.)
Blanshard, Paul. *Democracy and Empire in the Caribbean.* (New York, 1947.)
Bunau-Varilla, Philippe. *Panama, the Creation, Destruction, and Resurrection.* (New York, 1914.)
——. *The Great Adventure of Panama.* (New York, 1920.)
——. *From Panama to Verdun.* (Philadelphia, 1940.)
Burr, Robert N. *Colombia and International Cooperation, 1920-1929.* (Philadelphia: University of Pennsylvania microfilm, 1948.)
Castillero Reyes, Ernesto J. *El Profeta Panamá y su gran traición; el tratado del Canal y la intervención de Bunau-Varilla en su confección.* (Panamá, 1936.)
——. *La Universidad Interaméricana. Historia de sus antecedentes y fundación.* (Panamá, 1943.)
Childs, James B. *The Memorias of the Governments of Central America and the Antilles.* (Washington, 1932.)
Colunge, Guillermo. *The Panama Republic.* (Seville, 1929.)
Cooper, John C. *Air Law—International.* (Princeton, N. J., 1950.)
Core, Sue Pearl. *Panama, Yesterday and Today.* (New York, 1945.)
Cosentini, Francesco. *Los tratados y las convenciónes de la Zoña del Canal de Panamá—Las Bases Equitativas de un Nuevo Tratado.* (Panamá, 1928.)
Crowther, Samuel. *The Romance and Rise of the American Tropics —Colombia and Central America.* (New York, 1929.)

Davies, Howell, ed. *The South American Handbook 1946.* (London, 1946.)
Dimock, Marshall E. *Government Operated Enterprises in the Panama Canal Zone.* (Chicago, 1934.)
Duggan, Laurence. *The Americas—The Search for Hemispheric Security.* (New York, 1949.)
Duggan, Stephen. *The Two Americas, An Interpretation.* (New York, 1934.)
DuVal, Miles P. *Cadiz to Cathay, The Story of the Long Struggle for a Waterway Across the American Isthmus.* (Palo Alto, 1940.)
——. *And the Mountains Will Move.* (Palo Alto, 1947.)
Escobar, Felipe J. *El legado de los proceres; ensayo historico-political sobre la naciónalidad Panameña.* (Panamá, 1930.)
Finch, George A., ed. *The International Conferences of American States: Supplement 1933-1940.* (New York, 1940.)
Fitzgibbon, Russell H., ed. *The Constitutions of the Americas.* (Chicago, 1948.)
Franck, Harry A. *The Pan American Highway from the Rio Grande to the Canal Zone.* (New York, 1940.)
Freehoff, Joseph C. *America and the Canal Title.* (New York, 1916.)
Gantenbein, James W. *The Evolution of Our Latin American Policy, A Documentary Record.* (New York, 1950.)
Garay, Narciso. *Panamá y las Guerras de los Estados Unidos.* (Panamá, 1930.)
Gayoso, Jesús Vázquez, ed. *Una Nación en Guerra.* (Panamá, 1942.)
Goytía, Victor F. *El Liberalismo y la Constitución.* (Panamá, 1945.)
——. *La Función Geografica del Istmo.* (Panamá, 1947.)
——. *Bases y Doctrinas de Derecho Publico.* (Panamá, 1948), 2 vols.
——. *Mi Aporte—a la jurisprudencia.* (Panamá, 1949.)
Graell, C. Arrocha. *Historia de la independencia de Panamá, sus antecedentes y sus causas, 1821-1903.* (Panamá, 1933.)
Haas, William H. *The American Empire.* (Chicago, 1940.)
Hancock, Ralph. *The Rainbow Republics—Central America.* (New York, 1947.)
Harding, Earl. *In Justice to the United States—A Settlement With Colombia.* (New York, 1914.)
Hilton, Ronald, ed. *Hispanic Source Materials in the United States.* (Toronto, 1942.)

———. *Who's Who in Latin America, Part II—Central America and Panama.* (Palo Alto, Calif., 1945.)
Howard, Harry N. *Military Government in the Panama Canal Zone.* (Norman, Okla., 1931.)
Humphrey, John P. *The Inter-American System; A Canadian View.* (Toronto, 1942.)
Inman, Samuel Guy. *Building an Inter-American Neighborhood.* (New York, 1937.)
Ireland, Gordon. *Boundaries, Possessions, and Conflicts in Central and North America and the Caribbean.* (Cambridge, 1941.)
James, Preston. *Latin America.* (New York, 1942.)
Kelchner, Warren H., ed. *Inter-American Conferences, 1826-1933, Chronological and Classified Lists.* (Washington, 1933.)
———. *Latin American Relations with the League of Nations.* (Boston, 1930.)
Latané, John H. *The United States and Latin America.* (New York, 1928.)
Loewenstein, Karl, ed. Comité Consultivo de Emergencia para la defensa politica publicación, *Legislación para la Defensa Politica, en las Repúblicas Américanas.* (Montevideo, 1947), 2 vols.
McCain, William D. *The United States and the Republic of Panama.* (Durham, N. C., 1937.)
MacDonald, Austin F. *Latin American Politics and Government.* (New York, 1949.)
Mack, Gerstle. *The Land Divided, A History of the Panama Canal and Other Isthmian Projects.* (New York, 1944.)
Mansfield, Michael J. *The Panama Bases, Report of an Inquiry into Rejection of an Agreement on.* (Washington, 1948.)
Masters, Ruth T., ed. Carnegie Endowment for International Peace, *Handbook of International Organizations in the Americas.* (New York, 1945.)
Medina, Leandro. *Límité Oriental de Panamá.* (Bogotá, 1913.)
Méndez Pereira, Octavio. *Justo Arosemena, 1817-1896.* (Panamá, 1919.)
———. *Acción Democrática Internacional, Tres Fechas.* (Panamá, 1943.)
———, ed. *Antologia del Canal, 1914-1939.* (Panamá, 1939.)
Miner, Dwight C. *The Fight for the Panama Route.* (New York, 1940.)
Minter, John E. *The Chagres, River of Westward Passage.* (New York, 1948.)
Moore, John Bassett. *Digest of International Law as Embodied in*

Diplomatic Discussions and Treaties. (Washington, 1906), 8 vols.
Moore, J. Hampton. *With Speaker Cannon Through the Tropics.* (Philadelphia, 1907.)
Morison, Samuel E. *The Battle of the Atlantic.* (New York, 1947.)
Myers, Denys P. *Handbook of the League of Nations.* (New York, 1935.)
National Foreign Trade Council. *Economic Proposals for Consideration of the Ninth International Conference of American States.* (New York, 1947.)
Normano, John F. *The Struggle for South America.* (Boston, 1931.)
Notter, Harley A. *The Origins of the Foreign Policy of Woodrow Wilson.* (Baltimore, 1937.)
Padelford, Norman J. *The Panama Canal in Peace and War.* (New York, 1942.)
Padilla, Ezéquiel. *Free Men of America.* (Chicago, 1943.)
Parks, E. Taylor. *Colombia and the United States.* (Durham, N. C., 1935.)
Perkins, Dexter. *The United States and the Caribbean.* (Cambridge, 1947.)
Pozuelo A., José. *Por la Patria y por el amigo; testimonio relativo a los hechos que culminaron con el definitivo y feliz arreglo del problema fronterigo entre Costa Rica y Panamá.* (San José, Costa Rica, 1943.)
Quijano, M. de J. *En la Ruta Liberal y Democrática.* (Panamá, 1943.)
Quintanilla, Luis. *A Latin American Speaks.* (New York, 1943.)
Reynolds, T. H., ed. *The Progress of Pan Americanism.* (Washington, 1942.)
Rippy, J. Fred. *Latin America in World Politics.* (New York, 1928.)
Schuster, Edward. *A Guide to the Law and Legal Literature of the Central American Republics.* (New York, 1937.)
Scott, James B. *The Hague Peace Conferences of 1899 and 1907.* (Baltimore, 1909.)
———, ed. *The International Conferences of American States, 1889-1928.* (New York, 1931.)
Sherman, Charles P. *Roman Law in the Modern World.* (New Haven, 1922), 2 vols.
Skinner, Thomas and Co., Inc., publ. *The Yearbook of the West Indies and Countries of the Caribbean, 1948-1949.* (London, 1949.)
Smith, Darrell H. *The Panama Canal, Its History, Activities, and Organization.* (Baltimore, 1927.)
Stanley, Alexander O., ed. *A Geo-Economic Study of Latin America.* (New York, 1945.)

Stephens, H. M., and Bolton, H. E. *The Panama Congress—A Collection of Papers and Addresses on the Pacific Ocean in History.* (New York, 1917.)
Steward, Julian H., ed. *Handbook of the South American Indians,* Vol. IV. (Washington, 1948.)
Susto, Juan Antonio, ed. *Compilación, Indices, y Notas; Leyes expedidas por la Asamblea Nacional de Panamá, 1938.* (Panamá, 1939.)
———, and Castillero Reyes, Ernesto J., and Méndez Pereira, Octavio. *Panamá en la Gran Colombia.* (Panamá, 1939.)
Teeters, Negley K. *Penology from Panama to Cape Horn.* (Philadelphia, 1946.)
Tomlinson, Edward. *The Other Americans.* (New York, 1943.)
Valdés, Ramón M. *La independencia del Istmo de Panamá: sus antecedentes, sus causas, y su justificación.* (Panamá, 1903.)
Velarde, Fabian. *Analises de Nuevo Tratado.* (Panamá, 1927.)
Verrill, A. Hyatt. *Panama of Today.* (New York, 1927.)
Welles, Sumner. *The Time for Decision.* (New York, 1944.)
Whitaker, Arthur P. *The United States and South America—The Northern Republics.* (Cambridge, 1948.)
———, ed. *Inter-American Affairs—Annual Surveys Nos. 1-5.* (New York, 1942-46), 5 vols.
Williams, Mary W. *Anglo-American Isthmian Diplomacy, 1815-1915.* (London, 1915.)
———. *The People and Politics of Latin America,* rev. (Boston, 1945.)
Zea, Leopoldo. *Dos Etapas del Pensamiento en Hispanoamérica.* (Mexico City, 1949.)
Zeballos, E. S. *Conferencias internacionales Américanas, 1797-1910.* (Valencia, 1914.)
Zimmern, Alfred. *The League of Nations and the Rule of Law, 1918-1935.* (London, 1936.)

XI. Published Articles

Listed by Author

Alfaro, Ricardo J. "An American League of Nations," in *World Affairs,* September 1938.
———. "Addresses delivered at the Pan American Institute held at Oklahoma A. and M. College, Stillwater, Oklahoma, June 1941," printed in T. H. Reynolds, *The Progress of Pan Americanism, op. cit.,* p. 158.
Beichman, Arnold. "Red 'Phantom Fleet' Sails under Panama Flag: Boycott War Looms," *New Leader,* April 15, 1950.
Berguido, Carlos, Jr. "The Rights of a Seaman on a Ship under

Panamanian Registry," *Temple University Law Quarterly,* Philadelphia, Vol. XIX, No. 4, April 1946.

Bidwell, P. H. "Good Neighbors in the War and After," *Foreign Affairs,* Vol. XXI, April 1943.

Breece, Laurence M. "R. P. Merchant Marine is a Real Asset," the *Panama Star and Herald,* March 2, 1950.

Buell, Raymond Leslie. "Panama and the United States," *Foreign Policy Reports,* Vol. VII, No. 23, January 20, 1932.

Castillero Reyes, Ernesto J. "Los Precursores Panameños de Bolívar," *Boletín de la Academia Panameña de la Historia,* Ano. VI, No. 16-19, 1938.

Duggan, Stephen. "Latin America, the League, and the United States," *Foreign Affairs,* Vol. XII, January, 1934.

Fenwick, Charles G. "The Inter-American Conference for the Maintenance of Peace," *American Journal of International Law,* Vol. 31, 1937.

———. "The American Republics and International Law," *Bulletin of the Pan American Union,* April 14, 1947.

———. "The Pact of Bogotá and other Juridical Decisions of the Ninth Conference," *Bulletin of the Pan American Union,* Vol. 82, August 1948.

Galloway, Clark H. "Canal Zone Workers like their U.S. Shops," *The United States News and World Report,* December 3, 1948.

Garay, Narciso. "Les Relations exterieures et le statut international de Panama," *Séances et Travaux,* Paris, February 1929.

Humphrey, John P. "Argentina's Diplomatic Victory," *Canadian Forum,* Vol. XXI, March 1942.

Inman, Samuel Guy. "The Lima Conference and the Totalitarian Issue," *Annals of the American Academy of Political Science,* Vol. 204, July 1939.

Llano, Antonio. "A Colombian View of the Treaty," *New York Times,* March 13, 1917.

Lleras, Alberto. "The Bogotá Conference," *Bulletin of the Pan American Union,* Vol. 82, June 1942.

Marden, Luis. "Panama, Bridge of the World," *National Geographic Magazine,* November 1941.

Martin, Laurence and Silvia, "Nazi Intrigues in South America," *American Mercury,* Vol. LIII, July 1941.

Mason, Carol Y., and Rowlands, Adagrace. "Panama Canal Traffic," *Economic Geography,* Vol. 14, 1935.

Munro, Dana G. "The Mexico City Conference and the Inter-American System," *State Department Bulletin,* Vol. XII, April 8, 1945.

Murkland, H. B. "Attack Stirs Costa Rica," *Current History,* September 1942.

———. "Hispanic America and the War," *Current History*, February 1942.
Norton, H. K. "Why Britishers in Panama?," *World's Work*, November 1930.
Padilla, Ezéquiel. "The American System and the World Organization," *Foreign Affairs*, October 1945.
Price, A. Grenfell. "White Settlement in the Canal Zone," *Geographic Review*, Vol. 25, 1935.
Reisel, Victor. "The Labor Front," *Philadelphia Inquirer*, February 10, 1949.
Rippy, J. Fred. "Political Issues in Panama Today," *Current History*, Vol. XXVIII, 1928.
Seegers, Scott. "The World's Best Business Set-Up," *Inter-American Magazine*, August 1946.
Shallet, Sidney. "Can We Defend the Panama Canal?," *Saturday Evening Post*, October 9, 1948.
Shirer, W. L. "Hitler's Latin American Front," *The Nation*, Vol. CLIV, April 18, 1942.
Sohn, Louis B. "The Development of International Law—Declaration on the Rights and Duties of States," *American Bar Association Journal*, August 1949.
Steinberg, Morton C. "Sea Level Canal a Vital Defense Need," *Philadelphia Sunday Inquirer*, December 26, 1948.
Stirling, Matthew W. "Exploring the Past in Panama," *National Geographic Magazine*, March 1949.
———, and Stewart, Richard H. "Exploring Ancient Panama by Helicopter," *National Geographic Magazine*, February 1950.
Stout, R. L. "The League and the Panama Treaty," *The Independent*, Vol. CXVIII, 1927.
Vásquez Hernandez, Publio A. "La Personalidad internacional de Panamá," *Boletín de la Academia Panameña de Historia*, Ano. I, 1933.

XII. PUBLISHED LETTER

From Enrique A. Jiménez, former President of the Republic of Panama, printed in the *Saturday Evening Post*, November 13, 1948.

XIII. OTHER PUBLISHED ARTICLES

"Latin America After the War," *Living Age*, Vol. XXIII, July 2, 1921.
"Latin America and the League of Nations," *Current History*, Vol. 28, May 1923.
"Latin America's Attitude toward the League of Nations," *Current History*, Vol. 25, February 1923.

"Nazidom at Lima," *New Republic*, December 7, 1938.
"Panama: Arias Pro-Axis?," *Time*, December 30, 1940.
"Panama: Arnulfo Again," *Time*, December 5, 1949.
"Panama: Better Feeling," *Newsweek*, April 25, 1949.
"Panama: Hail to the Chief," *Time*, November 28, 1949.
"Panama: No Emparedados," *Time*, April 18, 1949.
"Panama: Plotter from Texas," *Newsweek*, May 2, 1949.
"Panama: Protocol," *Time*, June 13, 1949.
"Panama: Three Presidents," *Newsweek*, December 5, 1949.
"Panamanian Bonds," *Inter-American Magazine*, May 1944.
"Plans of the Atomic Age for the Big Ditch," *Philadelphia Inquirer*, November 10, 1946.

XIV. MAGAZINES AND PERIODICALS

American Bar Association. *Program of the 72nd Annual Meeting at St. Louis*, September 5-9, 1949.
American Judicature Society, *Journal*, Vol. 32, No. 6. (Ann Arbor, Michigan.)
Hispanic American Review. (Durham, N. C.) Individual citations in appropriate footnotes.
Inter-American Magazine. (Washington, D. C. and New York.) Individual citations appear in footnotes.
Newsweek. (Dayton, Ohio.) Individual citations in footnotes.
Panama Canal and Railroad, *Panama Canal Record*. Vol. 10 of 1916-17. (Ancon, C. Z., 1918.)
Sociedad Panameña de Derecho Internacional. *Annuario de la Sociedad, 1931-1933*. (Panamá, 1933.)
Time. (Chicago, Illinois.) Individual citations in footnotes.

XV. NEWSPAPERS

Individual citations appear in appropriate footnotes.
Chicago Daily News. Chicago, Illinois.
El Diario Nacional. Panama, R. P.
La Estrella de Panamá, and *The Star and Herald*. Panama, R. P.
New York Herald. New York, N. Y.
New York Times. New York, N. Y.
New York World. New York, N. Y.
Panama American. Panama, R. P.
Philadelphia Evening Bulletin. Philadelphia, Pa.
Philadelphia Inquirer. Philadelphia, Pa.
The Evening Star. Washington, D. C.
The Morning Journal. Panama, R. P.

INDEX

Absolute Non-Intervention, doctrine of, 22, 79, 83, 127
Alfaro, Horacio F., 65
Alfaro, Ricardo J., 34, 54, 61, 73, 77, 83, 107, 149, 162; at Havana 1928 Conference, 75-76; at Petropolis 1947 Conference, 132; at Bogotá in 1948, 134, 137, 138; work on U.N. Declaration on Rights and Duties of States, 154-57, 158
Amador, Manuel, 27
Amador, Raoul, 57, 65
Argentina, 28, 44, 82, 91, 92; at Rio in 1942, 98-99; "Argentine Question" at Chapultepec, 128-29; at San Francisco in 1945, 149-50
Arias, Arnulfo, 18, 20, 109-10, 158, 168, 174, 175, 176, 180, 181, 185n
Arias, Harmodio, 56, 57, 65, 80, 83, 92, 109, 158
Arosemena, Alcibíades, 176
Arosemena, Juan D., 61, 79, 92, 93, 109
Arosemena, Justo, 26
Atlantic City, 1943 Conference on Relief and Rehabilitation (UNRRA), 124, 145
Austria-Hungary: recognizes Panama independence, 16; Panama declares war against, 44; Nazi seizure of Austria, 84, 88

Balboa, Vasco Núñez, 1, 74

Bases, *see* Defense Bases
Bemis, Samuel Flagg, 30, 72
Berguido, Carlos, Jr., 178, 180
"Black Lists," in World War I, 47-48
Bogotá, 2, 34, 35, 134; Conference of 1948 (Ninth International Conference of American States), 134-39; rioting during, 138
Bolívar, Simón, 2, 3, 25, 74
Bolivarian Commemoration Congress of 1926, 2, 74, 81, 93
"Bolivarian" countries, 2, 147
Boyd, Jorge E., 96, 125, 151, 162
Brazil, 82, 92, 99, 125, 168; recognition of Panama and Treaty of Arbitration with, 17; claim for permanent seat in League of Nations, 58
Bretton Woods Monetary and Banking Conference of 1944, 124, 145-46
Brin, Carlos, 141n, 160, 161, 182
Buenos Aires: Fourth International Conference of American States, 31-32; Inter-American Conference for the Maintenance of Peace, 80, 83, 88, 89
Bunche, Ralph, 154
"Bunker System," World War I, 45, 46, 47
Burgos, Antonio, 55, 56, 58

Chanis, Daniel, 20, 158, 174, 177
Chapultepec, Inter-American Conference on Problems of War and Peace, 1945, 124-31, 148, 149, 150, 151, 157
Chicago Civil Aviation Conference, 1944, 146-47
Chile, 61, 82, 92, 97, 98, 99
Clark Memorandum, 78, 79
Colombia, 2, 14, 15, 16, 17, 25, 26, 82, 92, 98, 131, 132, 138, 147; and Thomson-Urrutia Convention, 32-35
Colón, R. P., 7, 9, 46, 47, 53, 63, 118, 182; descriptions of, 3, 5
Commissaries of the U.S. government in Canal Zone, 8, 63, 83, 159, 169
Communism in Panama, 168-71, 179, 182
Coolidge, Calvin, 55, 73, 75, 76
Costa Rica, 16, 82; boundary dispute with Panama, 59-62

David, R. P., 10, 47, 139; description of city, 4-5
Davis, Monnett B., 173, 182
Defense Bases, World War II, 19, 110, 171-73, 158, 160, 161
Díaz Arosemena, Domingo, 20, 173, 175
Dollar Diplomacy, 31, 73
Drago Doctrine, 27-30
Drago, Luis, 28, 30
Drummond, Sir Eric, 60, 65
Dulles, John Foster, 43
Dumbarton Oaks Conference, 1944, 125, 126, 148, 150

Estrada Doctrine, 136, 137

Fábrega, Octavio, 97, 98, 103n
Financial and Economic Advisory Committee, 94-95, 99, 130
France, 16, 42, 95

Garay, Narciso, 51n, 56, 57, 65, 74, 83, 92, 93, 95
Germans in Panama, 5, 41, 42, 45, 48, 89-90, 108-9, 112
Germany, 16, 34, 41, 45, 84, 89, 90, 93, 99; Panama at war with, in 1917, 44; Panamanian declaration of war against, in World War II, 111; Caribbean U-Boat blitz, 114, 116, 119
Gondra Treaty, 78
Good Neighbor Policy, 79, 81, 83
Gran Colombia, see Colombia
Great Britain, 14, 15, 16, 41, 45, 146; trade interests in Panama, 9-10; World War II operations, 106; member of "Big Three," 147, 149; economic pressure on Argentina in World War II, 128

Hague Conference of 1907, 27, 28-31, 39
Harding, Warren G., 54, 55, 60, 73
Havana: Sixth International Conference of American States in 1928, 74-77; Second Meeting of the Foreign Ministers of the American States, 95-97
Hay-Bunau-Varilla Treaty, 15, 16, 20, 40, 53, 63, 80, 105, 152
Hay-Herran Treaty, 15
Hay, John, 26

INDEX 205

Hay-Pauncefote Treaty, 14
Hines-Jiménez Treaty, 172-74
Hispanidad, 18, 19, 109-10, 118, 171, 173, 175
Hoover, Herbert, 21, 78
Hot Springs Food and Agriculture Conference of 1943, 124, 145
Hughes, Charles E., 34, 60, 72, 73
Hull-Alfaro Treaty, 22, 80, 81, 83, 105, 111, 182
Hull, Cordell, 79, 91, 111

Indians: in Panama today, 3, 5; San Blas and Guayami pre-Colombian civilizations, 4
Inter-American Conferences, see Bogotá, Buenos Aires, Chapultepec, Havana, Lima, Montevideo, Mexico City, Petropolis, Rio de Janeiro, Santiago, Washington
Inter-American System, 21, 25-35, 72-87, 88-104, 124-43, 183
Inter-American University, 82, 91, 100
International Labor Organization, 161, 177-80
Italy, 42, 90, 99, 109; Panamanian declaration of war against, in 1941, 111; seizure of Italian shipping, 107, 120n

Japan, 41, 62, 93, 107; Panama enters World War II after Pearl Harbor attack by, 111; war plans aimed at Panama and Canal, 97, 112-13, 116-17
Jiménez, Enrique A., 145, 158, 159, 172
Jiménez, Roberto, 125, 134, 149, 151

Kellogg-Alfaro Treaty, 62-65
Kellogg-Briand Pact, 78
Kellogg, Frank B., 74-75
Korean War of 1950, 159-61, 181

la Guardia, Ernesto, 173
la Guardia, Ricardo de, 110, 111, 112, 114
Lansing-Morales Protocol, 40, 49n, 106
Lansing, Robert, 43, 45
Larreta Doctrine, 136, 137, 138
Latin American Bureau of the League of Nations, 59, 66
League of Nations, 34, 53-71, 127
Lefevre, José, 32, 74, 91, 132
Lesseps, Ferdinand de, 15, 42
Lima, Eighth International Conference of American States, 1938, 89-92, 109

Méndez Pereira, Octavio, 65, 149, 151, 165n
Merchant Marine of Panama, 107, 108, 110, 115, 116, 177-180
Mestizos, 4, 170
Mexico, 30, 44, 92, 98, 125, 132, 171
Mexico City: Second International Conference of American States, 1902, 26; Inter-American Conference on Problems of War and Peace, 1945, see Chapultepec
Ministers of Foreign Affairs of the American Republics, meetings of, see Panama City, Havana, and Rio de Janeiro
Monroe Doctrine, 31
Montevideo, Seventh International Conference of Ameri-

can States, 1933, 79-80, 154
Morales, Eusebio A., 54, 64
Morison, Samuel E., 112-13, 117

New Granada, *see* Colombia
Nicaragua, 14, 76, 174

Obaldía, José Domingo de, 26, 27, 31
Obaldía, Manuel, 31

Padilla, Ezequiel, 97, 98, 99
Panama Canal, 7, 8, 14, 21, 22, 39, 46, 72, 96, 105, 114, 152, 169, 170
Panama Canal Zone, status and sovereignty over, 40, 41, 54, 64, 105-7, 152-54, 158, 161
Panama City: descriptions of, 3, 5, 9; Bolivarian Congress of 1926, 74; Inter-American Educational Conference of 1943, 100; municipal bonds, 118; First Consultative Meeting of the Foreign Ministers of the American States, 1939, 92-95
Pan American Highway, 10, 82-83, 139
Pershing, John J., 62
Petropolis, Brazil, Conference of 1947, *see* Rio de Janeiro
Pitman, Key, 105, 106
Porras, Belisario, 29, 30, 31, 32, 65, 72
Porter Proposition, 30, 76

Quijano, M. de J., 90, 118, 121n, 162

Remón, José A., 117, 176
Revolutions: of 1903, 14, 27, 53; of 1941, 110, 111; of 1949, 168, 175, 181; of 1951, 175-76, 181
Rio de Janeiro: Third International Conference of American States, 1906, 26-29; Rio Commission of Jurists, 31, 75, 76; Third Consultative Meeting of the Foreign Ministers of American States, 1942, 97-99, 124; Inter-American Conference for the Maintenance of Continental Peace and Security at Petropolis, 1947, 131-34
Rippy, J. Fred, 53, 60
Rockefeller, Nelson, 150
Rodriguez, Cristobal, 65, 66
Rodriguez-Garay Convention, 61
Roosevelt Corollary, 28, 78
Roosevelt, Franklin D., 78, 80, 107, 113
Roosevelt, Theodore, 16, 23n
Root, Elihu, 28, 29
Rubber, World War II development in Panama, 118
Russia, 16, 29; Panamanian shipping used to carry lend-lease supplies to, 115-16; Soviet activity in the U.N., 147, 155, 156; charged with inspiring Bogotá riots in 1948, 138; present attitude of Panama toward, 182

Saavedra Lamas, Carlos, 78, 89
San Francisco, Conference for United Nations Organization, 1945, 149-51, 157, 158
Santiago, Chile, Fifth International Conference of American States, 1923, 2, 35, 73-74, 77
Soviet Union, *see* Russia

INDEX

Spain, 55, 82; influence of Falange in Panama, 90, 109, 171

Taft, William H., 31

Thomson-Urrutia Convention, 33-35

Truman, Harry S., 139, 170

United Fruit Company, 9, 50*n*

United Nations, 21, 67, 101, 127, 133, 144-66, 177, 180, 183

United Public Workers, 168, 171

United States of America: economic relations with Panama, 7-10; and Revolution of 1903, 15-17; position vis-à-vis R.P. foreign relations, 20-22; exercise of authority in Canal Zone, 40, 41, 54, 64, 105-7, 152-54, 158, 161; attitude of Panama towards, after World War I, 53-55; role in Costa Rica boundary dispute, 59-62; hostility toward, at Havana, 1928, 74-77; change in attitudes after 1930, 78-81; controversy over defense bases after World War II, 171-73; status of relations with Panama in "Cold War," 181-82. *See also* World Wars I and II, Commissaries, Drago Doctrine, Defense Bases, Hay-Bunau-Varilla Treaty, etc.

Valdés, Ramón M., 83

Venezuela, 2, 42, 46, 82, 98, 125, 147

Versailles Conference, 1918-19, 49, 55-56, 89

Washington, D.C.: First International Conference of American States, 1889, 25, 26; Arbitration Conference, 1929, 77

Welles, Sumner, 81, 91, 92, 98

White, Edward Douglas, 59, 60

Wilson, Woodrow, 40, 49

World War I, 39-52, 89, 107

World War II, 66, 92, 105-23, 160